Hiring, Training, and Supervising Library Shelvers

ALA Guides for the Busy Librarian

Writing and Publishing: The Librarian's Handbook,
edited by Carol Smallwood

Hiring, Training, and Supervising Library Shelvers

Patricia Tunstall

American Library Association
Chicago   2010

Patricia Tunstall is an information assistant at Indian Trails Public Library in Wheeling, Illinois. She spends most of her time at the reference desk helping patrons with their questions and their leisure reading choices. She was first employed as a page at Indian Trails and subsequently as the supervisor of pages and shelving. Since receiving a teaching certificate from Nottingham University in England, she has held jobs in a variety of fields. She is an occasional contributor of articles to library publications.

Library of Congress Cataloging-in-Publication Data

Tunstall, Patricia.
    Hiring, training, and supervising library shelvers / Patricia Tunstall.
      p. cm. — (ALA guides for the busy librarian)
    Includes index.
    ISBN 978-0-8389-1010-8 (alk. paper)
    1. Library pages.   2. Library personnel management.   I. Title.
  Z682.4.L49T86 2010
  023'.3—dc2   2009017002

ISBN-13: 978-0-8389-1010-8

Printed in the United States of America
14 13 12 11 10   5 4 3 2 1

CONTENTS

Additional material can be found on the book's website, at www.ala.org/editions/extras/tunstall10108. Look for website material wherever you see this symbol: **WEB**

PREFACE

There is more than one way to end up as a supervisor of library pages. You might be a librarian whose job description has recently been expanded to include looking after the shelvers in your own department. Or you might be a former shelver who, after a few years of giving first-class service, has been asked to take charge of your fellow workers. Whichever route you took to get here, you are probably wishing that you had more experience managing other people or some relevant training. Some of you are wishing you could have both, and instantly.

Hiring, Training, and Supervising Library Shelvers has the practical advice that you are looking for. It is based on my own experiences both as a page and then as a supervisor in a suburban public library where, for three years, I was in charge of a pool of over twenty pages. As I'm sure you are aware, the turnover of those who tote carts and lift books can be high, and so I frequently had the opportunity to hone my interviewing, hiring, and training skills. In this book, I am passing on all that I learned about what works well, and also admitting to a mistake or two that I relate in the hope that you won't have to make them.

Shelvers are vital to libraries, and yet they often receive little in the way of recognition from the upper ranks of management. We all know that if the army of people who sort and put away materials did not come in and do their jobs, the effects would be felt immediately throughout the library. In spite of their importance, it is not unusual to hear shelvers referred to as a vaguely troublesome bunch whose main claim to fame is their high rate of turnover. I believe we will all benefit if more attention is paid to the way these essential workers are selected and trained.

Use the chapter titles to find the topics that interest you the most. I have included some forms—testing and evaluation materials for the interviewing process and logs for keeping track of daily page activities—in the appendix of this book. Other supervisors in neighboring library districts and I have thoroughly tried and tested these materials.

I have also included a chapter on how to move multiple collections at once within a building or from one building to another. As a shelving supervisor, it will certainly be to your advantage to have a grasp of how major reorganizations can be done. My step-by-step guide will enable you to complete these tasks with a minimum of both tears and misshelved items.

Throughout this book, I have used the terms *shelver* and *page* to describe someone who is hired principally to sort and shelve returned library materials.

I am confident that you will find this manual useful, and I am very happy to put my experience at your disposal.

ACKNOWLEDGMENTS

This book is based on my article, "The Accidental Supervisor," which was published in the May/June 2006 issue of *Public Libraries* magazine. It also includes material from my article "Let's Move: How to Move Your Collections without Hiring Movers (and without Spending a Fortune!)," which appeared in *The U*N*A*B*A*S*H*E*D Librarian* in 2001.

My thanks to Indian Trails Public Library District in Wheeling, Illinois, for allowing me to make use of its Page Skills Test in this book.

I thank Carol Dolin and Rosa Lloyd for their help and advice during the writing of both this book and the article that preceded it. I hired both of them as shelvers, and they each succeeded me as the shelving supervisor at Indian Trails Public Library.

I also thank all of the shelvers I hired and all shelving supervisors I have met. I learned something from each one of them.

I owe many thanks to Sally Decker Smith, a fellow writer, for her unfailing encouragement and support.

Finally, thanks to my husband, John, for understanding that people who write spend a lot of time in rooms by themselves.

CHAPTER ONE

LOOKING FOR RECRUITS

The people you supervise are likely to fall into two distinct groups as far as length of service goes. It's not unusual for established libraries to have a core of mature pages who have been at the library since time immemorial and know the collections well. The rest of the shelvers are likely to be much younger—high school or college students, for instance—and they typically stay for no more than two years. This means that every couple of months, you may find yourself looking for new employees. During an economic downturn, there may be a lot of people dropping in to the library and filling out applications in the hope that a position opens up. In this case, you will have no trouble finding candidates to interview. Times are not always hard, though, so sometimes you will have to seek out recruits. Your advertising budget is likely to be very small or nonexistent, so here are some suggestions for spreading the word:

- Existing pages may have friends or siblings who are looking for work, and asking them first is a good idea. But be aware that many libraries have rules about employing people from the same household at the same time.
- Posting the job opening on your library's public website may net you some applicants.
- Putting up notices around the building can be productive, as there always seem to be a few patrons looking for a job. (See the vacant position sign in the appendix.)
- If your library has a bookmobile, display a notice on it.
- Ask high school career counselors to publicize job openings.
- The local home schooling association may be receptive to letting its members know you are looking for responsible teens.
- Senior centers often have programs that help their more active members find jobs and are worth contacting.

- If your library has contacts with leaders of ethnic groups in your community, let them know that you would welcome qualified applicants.

During my time as a page supervisor, I developed a working relationship with a nearby mental health center. My contact was a social worker looking for jobs in a nurturing environment for clients who were recovering from depression and other illnesses. The center provided a job coach for each candidate it sent us. The coach sat in on the interview, mostly offering just silent support to the applicant. When I hired someone from the center, the coach accompanied the person for his first three or four shifts and helped him settle into the routine of being an employee again. This arrangement worked well for all of us. I did not lower my hiring standards at all, and the library gained some top-notch pages. Several of these shelvers stayed with us for a number of years, and two are with us to this day.

One group of would-be pages never seemed to be in short supply: eager 14-year-olds looking for a job as soon as dawn breaks on their birthday. Unfortunately I could rarely offer them anything. Many states have strict labor laws governing the hiring of people under the age of 16. (Check your state labor laws on this issue.) In my state, Illinois, they may not work past 7:00 p.m. during the school year. Since the library closes at 9:00 p.m. and it is essential to have pages in the building for the cleanup and closing procedures, I could have only one 14-year-old on staff at a time. It was a shame to keep turning these young people away, but quite a few did come back and try again when they turned 16.

Whenever anyone came to the library and asked about openings in the page pool, I always spoke to them and answered their questions about what the work of a shelver involves. I then invited them to fill out an application even when I was not hiring. In that way, I always had one or two people to contact when I had an opening.

You should have a clear idea of what your requirements are for shelvers. Here is a basic list that you can adapt:

- usually must be at least 16 years old
- must have the ability to arrange items by alphabet
- must have the ability to arrange items in number order
- must have an eye for detail
- must be fit enough to handle a loaded book cart
- can take instructions with good humor
- works well with others

A completed application form is not going to tell you all you need to know about a potential employee (that's what interviews are for), but it can help you decide if it is worth asking this person to come in for an interview and then try and determine if the applicant will be a good fit for the job opening.

Look for the following points on the application:

- The person's writing is neat and readable.
- All required sections are filled out.
- The employment history seems complete.
- The person has useful skills (perhaps he or she is computer literate and speaks a second language).
- The applicant uses complete sentences on the application form where appropriate.

Anyone you hire will require a good deal of your time and effort to train, so try to assess which applicants are likely to stay with you for a couple of years if you take them on. There are clues to look for, and they are often found in the section of the application form where candidates are invited to give any other information that they think you will find of interest. I often found that phrases like these were a good sign:

- "I love libraries."
- "I have always wanted to work in a library."
- "I am a lifelong reader and love books."

People who are already fans of the library will start out with some basic knowledge of how materials are organized and are likely to appreciate the need for keeping everything in good order.

An explanation of how an applicant intends to fit the library working hours in with the rest of her life is always useful and encouraging—for example:

- "I am taking classes during the day but am free to work evenings and weekends."
- "I have another part-time job, but I would be able to fit in my hours at the library too."
- "I would be available during the hours that my children are in school."
- "I am a retiree and can be very flexible about working hours."

People who have given some thought to how a part-time job will affect their lives are usually worth interviewing.

If an applicant gives a fairly lengthy list of previous full-time jobs but no clear reason for leaving the last one, be cautious, especially if the person gives any of the following reasons for applying:

- "I need a job."
- "I need the money."
- "I have bills to pay."

There is nothing wrong at all with wanting a job for those reasons, but a low-paid, part-time position is probably not going to meet these needs. Someone who was hired and was seeking a living wage would not likely stay with you for long.

Don't feel that you are obliged to see everyone who hands in an application. Use the forms to narrow the field. Your time is valuable, and you cannot afford to spend hours with people who will not meet your requirements.

Once you have decided which applicants to interview, try to set up these appointments close together. If you see half a dozen people in the space of a couple of days, you will be able to keep your impressions of them fresh in your mind, and this will help when it comes to deciding which one to hire.

If you leave a phone message with someone offering an interview and the person does not reply, I advise against calling a second time. You want to see only the people who are sufficiently enthusiastic about the job and well organized enough to get back to you promptly.

Sometimes, in spite of all your efforts to attract new people, you will suffer a drought of suitable candidates. I have two pieces of advice for anyone in this situation. First, do not panic. Make sure everyone in the library knows that you are temporarily short of staff. Meet with staff in other departments and explain why restocking times may fall below their expectations. Then reach agreement on which materials should have priority for shelving. Let it be known that you will very much appreciate any help other staff can give. I always found that many of the staff at the reference desks were more than willing to sort a cart of materials or shelve in the areas closest to their stations during the quieter times of the day.

The second piece of my advice is never to give in to the temptation of hiring the first breathing body who comes through the door. Always ask yourself if you would even be considering giving this person employment if you were not shorthanded. If you do hire someone out of desperation, you will end up regretting your choice for the next several weeks or even months. Holding out for someone who truly meets all your requirements is a far better way of going about hiring employees.

CHAPTER TWO

INTERVIEWING AND HIRING

INTERVIEWING

If you are on the interviewer's side of the table for the first time, you may be a little hesitant about your ability to decide which applicant to hire. If you don't want to go it alone at first, by all means seek help. Are there staff who have consistently hired people who are good at their jobs and pleasant to work with? If so, these staff obviously have skills that could benefit you. Don't be shy about asking for help. Most people are flattered to be asked to act as a mentor, and they may be willing to sit with you for your first couple of interviews until you gain confidence. If you are working in a smaller organization and need to be self-reliant, I suggest you consult some of the many books and DVDs on the subject of interviewing. Doing some research will give you an overview of what's involved in the process and help you form your own general ideas on how to approach it. The advice in this chapter is based on the experience I gained during interviews with a few hundred potential shelvers.

The interview is your opportunity to identify people who can be trained quickly to be efficient shelvers. You are also looking for people who will fit into your existing team of workers and the library environment.

Although the physical requirements of shelving rule out some people who are not sufficiently agile, a condition such as deafness need not be a barrier. I hired a profoundly deaf person some years ago. It was apparent during the interview that her lip-reading skills were very good, and I felt confident that we would be able to communicate well during her training and under normal working conditions. That turned out to be the case. If she needed to "speak" to me by telephone, we used the TDD system. Now, of course, it is much easier to accommodate a person with hearing difficulties with the advent of text messaging, instant messaging, and other applications.

I recommend you use a list of questions that you have prepared in advance and take notes on each candidate's answers. Paying attention to details at this stage will save you time and trouble later. Figure 2.1 lists some questions that I found useful, and the appendix contains additional interview questions.

FIGURE 2.1   *INTERVIEW QUESTIONS*

1. Due to child labor laws, individuals under 16 years of age cannot work past 7:00 p.m. during the school year. Are you 16? If not, when will you be?
2. Why did you leave your last job?
3. Tell me about the most challenging aspect of your last job (or school life). How did you meet this challenge?
4. How would you rate yourself on attendance and punctuality?
5. The hours for this job are evenings and weekends during the school year. What days and hours within this time frame are most convenient for you?
6. Will you be able to work during those hours during the entire school year?
7. Are you willing to work evenings and weekends during the summer?
8. You would be required to work 24 hours within a two-week pay period and to schedule yourself so that there are no four-day gaps between workdays. Could you commit to this arrangement?
9. Employees in this job are required to push heavy carts and maneuver them in tight spaces. You may be asked to rearrange furniture for library program setups. You must be able to stretch and bend to reach high and low shelves. Do you have any physical limitations that would prevent you from meeting any of these requirements?
10. How do you think you would you handle a situation in which a patron made a mess of some books that you had just put away?
11. What would you do if a patron complained to you about library services or materials?
12. Why did you decide to apply for a job with this library?
13. What interests you most about this job?
14. One of the most important qualifications needed for this job is reliability. Tell me about a time in your past when you showed how reliable you can be.
15. Do you have any questions about the job or the library?

You will notice that some of the questions are slanted toward younger applicants and are not appropriate for everyone. Have a copy of the sheet of questions with you in the interview, and always jot down brief notes on it about the candidate's answers as you go along. This is especially important if you are going to speak to several interviewees and will not be making a decision until you've interviewed them all. Don't forget to write the applicant's name on the sheet. As you listen to a candidate's answers, try not to show what you are thinking. How would you feel if someone interviewing you began frowning or shaking his head while you were speaking? It's certain that you are going to have to turn down many more people than you offer jobs to, but you should give all candidates a hearing that they believe is fair and unbiased.

By the time you have used these questions a few times with candidates, you will probably have developed a pattern of your own. You will also discover which questions are most useful to you and can mark them in some way so that you can be sure you always ask them of every candidate you meet with. For example, you may prefer to put the questions you always ask at the top of this list so that each interview begins in the same way. I was not always concerned about the order in which I asked the questions. I found that if conversation was flowing during an interview, the answers to several of them would emerge in the natural course of things, and I just had to be sure to make notes.

Give all candidates a written test of their ability to alphabetize names and arrange Dewey numbers correctly. Even if an interview seems to be going splendidly and you are impressed with the candidate's educational background, personality, and communication skills, do not be tempted to drop this part of the interview process. You'll be surprised how many people who seem bright and capable lack these basic but essential skills. It's important to remember that hiring someone who is incapable of putting materials in alphabetical and numerical order will be a complete waste of your time and theirs.

The test shown in figure 2.2 has been given to page applicants at our library for as long as anyone can remember, and we have found it to be a reliable indicator of a candidate's future shelving prowess. (The appendix contains an alternative shelving quiz.) Don't forget to keep a master copy for yourself with the answers circled to save time when marking.

Always use a double safety net of the paper quiz followed by a practical test using a cart of fiction and nonfiction materials. I have had interviews in which candidates have correctly answered all of the questions on the written test but flunked the hands-on part. Some people even forgot to do anything at all with the large cart of books that I left sitting next to them. Books from the youth sections of the library are ideal for this part of the test because you can put a large number of items on the cart, both fiction and nonfiction, giving the candidates a thorough workout of their ability to put materials in order.

I always gave the written and practical tests at the end of the interview. Once I had given a brief explanation of what the written test required, I took candidates over to the cart of books I had previously set up and did my best to make sure that they understood exactly what I wanted them to do. Then I went away and left them to it. I always used an office or meeting room for the interview and test, so that the candidates could concentrate on what they were doing. I never set a time limit and always encouraged people to go at their own pace. Most managed to finish both tests in less than thirty

FIGURE 2.2 *PAGE SKILLS TEST* [WEB]

PART ONE: ALPHABETICAL

Name: _____   Date: _____

Circle the correct answer for each of the following questions.

When the following names are put in alphabetical order, which one will come second?

1. Marshall, Charles
2. Marshall, John
3. Marshall, Thomas Riley
4. Marshall, George Catlett
5. Marshall, James Wilson

When the following names are put in alphabetical order, which one will come fourth?

1. McCormick, Cyrus Hall
2. McCosh, James
3. McConnell, Francis J
4. McCormack, John
5. McCormick, Joseph Medill

When the following names are put in alphabetical order, which one will come third?

1. Harris, Chandler Joel
2. Henry, O
3. Harte, Bret
4. Hearn, Lafcadio
5. Hayne, Paul Hamilton

When the following titles are put in alphabetical order, which one will come first?

1. *The Raven*
2. *Bells*
3. *The Adventures of Robin Hood*
4. *The Sea Gypsy*
5. *The Pasture*

When the following names are put in alphabetical order, which one will come first?

1. Dickey, Herbert Spencer
2. Dickinson, John
3. Dickinson, Emily
4. Dickens, Charles
5. Dickenson, G. Lowes

Put the following list of words in alphabetical order. Number them from 1 to 5.

___ manse
___ manservant
___ mansard
___ mansion
___ manslaughter

PART TWO: NUMERICAL

Circle your answers.

If you arrange these two groups of numbers in order (starting with the lowest), which numbers will come third?

Group A	Group B
1. 870.5421	1. 896.0501
2. 870.5521	2. 896.0506
3. 860.5924	3. 896.0560
4. 870.5923	4. 896.0500
5. 870.5663	5. 897.0569

If you arrange these two groups of numbers in order (starting with the lowest), which numbers will come second?

Group C	Group D
1. 786.5301	1. 678.432
2. 786.5306	2. 658.432
3. 768.5304	3. 658.434
4. 786.5314	4. 658.424
5. 786.5214	5. 658.422

If you arrange these two groups of numbers in order (starting with the lowest), which ones will come fourth?

Group E	Group F
1. 352.548	1. 428.7654
2. 325.458	2. 428.6574
3. 355.584	3. 428.7465
4. 325.564	4. 428.7645
5. 325.546	5. 428.7653

Put the following two groups in order. Number them from 1to 5, beginning with the lowest.

Group G	Group H
___ 599.744	___ 398.378909
___ 599.7442	___ 398.379808
___ 599.743456	___ 398.3789065
___ 599.7446	___ 389.378909
___ 599.744193	___ 398.3789

minutes. On two occasions when an hour went by and the candidates did not emerge, I went back in to find them struggling with the paper quiz. In both cases, I let them bow out gracefully by asking if they thought they could complete the test if I gave them more time. The answer both times was no, and I then pointed out tactfully that I could consider their application complete only if the test was finished. After that, we were able to agree that perhaps working in a library wasn't suitable for them after all.

Another essential interviewing tool is a candidate evaluation sheet. You are looking for certain qualities and abilities in the people you interview, and you need a way to record how close each person comes to the standard you require. By using an evaluation sheet, you can translate your impressions of each candidate into a measurable score. Figure 2.3 shows the one that I used.

If you award up to 5 points in each category and then use the multipliers, the highest possible score is 75. To make good use of this assessment tool, decide on the lowest score that is acceptable to you and then never hire anyone who falls below it. I chose 65 as my standard. The score for accuracy will be based on how well the applicant performs the written and practical shelving tests. I suggest taking 1 point off for every two errors.

Communication skills become apparent as soon as you contact or meet the person:

- Did she fill out the application form clearly?
- Did she make sense when you spoke on the phone?
- Did she meet your eyes during your face-to-face conversation and smile when it was appropriate?
- Did she listen to and understand your questions during the interview, and were her answers appropriate?

FIGURE 2.3   *APPLICANT EVALUATION SHEET*   `WEB`

Name: _____   Date: _____
Position applied for: _____

	Rating (1–5)		Total
Accurate		x 5	
Communicates well		x 4	
Reliable		x 3	
Flexible		x 2	
Appearance		x 1	
Grand Total			

Communication skills are an important part of what you are looking for in a candidate. Shelvers must be able to listen to and understand instructions. They need to be able to speak to their colleagues about the tasks they have completed or are still working on. They also need to be able to respond politely and appropriately to questions from patrons or staff from other departments.

It's not easy to find out if someone you have just met is reliable, but there are indicators. For example, was the person on time for the interview? Was she able to give you an example of how she had behaved responsibly in the past?

When it comes to personal appearance, it's important not to be too judgmental. Look for neatness and cleanliness, reasonable standards to expect of any employee. Hairstyles, clothing choices, and body piercing indicate nothing at all about anybody's potential shelving ability. If a person shows up for an interview with a bare midriff or pants hanging low in the rear, you may want to point out that your library does have some dress standards that all staff members are expected to adhere to during working hours. You could have a copy of the regulations handy and ask all applicants if they are willing and able to comply.

You may feel that assessing candidates should be a process based on instinct and personal judgment and that it is somehow dehumanizing to attempt to reduce them to a score. But you are looking for people with definable and recognizable skills who will become assets to the library. Your potential employees' success and happiness in the job depend on their having specific aptitudes. You do all candidates a service by being methodical in your approach and using a range of tools to improve your chances of making sound choices. Being practical does not mean that you have to set your humanity aside. You will still need all your character reading abilities when it comes to deciding if a candidate with a high score also has the social skills needed to blend in well with your existing staff.

During the interview, it's vital to give your potential employees as much information as possible. Mention pay as early as possible. You don't want anyone to have any illusions about what they will be earning, but it doesn't all have to be bad news. Let them know how soon they could expect their first pay raise, and explain what their prospects for promotion might be. Then explain the basic requirements of the job. Be clear about the following requirements.

Hours

State the number of hours per week that the job entails and how many of those must be worked on evenings or weekends. If you don't intend to hire people on a seasonal basis, be sure to emphasize that the position is a year-round responsibility. This can often be an issue if you are in a region that has cold winters and you employ retirees. Imagine the disruption if two or three of your staff members suddenly announce in December that they will be spending the next three months in Florida.

I advise against interviewing high school students at the beginning of summer vacation because a high proportion of them are likely to want summer work only. If you ask them outright if they intend to continue working once school starts again, they may say yes but leave in the fall anyway, often due to parental pressure. You will have invested many hours of your time training them, only to have them leave just as they are becoming really useful. Wait until August when you will need to recruit in order to replace your high school shelvers who are going off to college.

When you are interviewing high school students, get as clear a picture as possible of the number of weekly commitments they have during the academic year. Ask them specifically if they will be available to work for the number of hours each week that you need at the times you require. Ask them to tell you about the after-school activities that they enjoy. If it turns out that they have soccer, debate, band, and choir all lined up for the next semester but are sure that they can fit work in somewhere, cross them off your list of potential employees. If they overload their schedule, something will have to be dropped, and it will more than likely be their job.

Physical Requirements

Applicants often don't realize that shelving and other page duties involve a lot of bending and lifting or that carts loaded with books can be very heavy. Be sure to ask them if they believe that they are capable of the physical effort required. Some supervisors ask candidates to push a cart loaded with books from one place to another in the library as part of the interview. It would make sense to avoid hiring anyone who mentions frequently suffering from painful muscle spasms in their back. In spite of asking what I thought were all the right questions, I still had someone quit halfway through the first day because the work was too strenuous.

Many people who apply for part-time jobs in libraries are under the impression that they are entering an environment that is quiet and sheltered from the outside world and that they are in for a relaxing time. You need to put everyone straight about this at the interview stage. Tell them plainly that shelving is a never-ending and fairly strenuous occupation and that the flow of returned materials does not stop.

Explain that shelvers need to turn up for their appointed shifts on time and without fail. Point out that they will be expected to complete a certain amount of work during each shift and that there is no time to read the books while putting them away. You should also point out that, in general, shelvers are expected to work in whatever section of the library you require. No one should leave an interview with the impression that they could come in and just work with the mysteries or the science fiction that they love. By speaking plainly to candidates about the requirements of the job, you lessen the risk of hiring someone who leaves on the first day because the job was not what he or she expected.

Being honest about the demands of the position does not mean that you cannot also highlight the pleasurable aspects of working in a library. Many people derive a great deal of satisfaction from working for an institution that serves their community and will enjoy being in a relatively tranquil environment.

HIRING

It is a good idea to hold off until the day after you have interviewed someone before offering that person a position, and you should certainly wait until you have seen all other candidates. Thank each person for coming, and let everyone know that they will hear from you regardless of the outcome.

Do not mark the written and practical tests until your applicants have left the building. If you evaluate a candidate's efforts while that person is still in the room, you may be tempted to tell her if she has done well. This may lead the candidate to expect a job offer, but if your next candidate is even better, you will have raised the first person's hopes for nothing. There is absolutely no point in pressuring yourself to make rapid decisions. I say this because I once hired someone on the spot and came to regret it. Would I have hired this person anyway a few days later? I cannot be certain that I would have done it differently, but after that experience, I always gave myself time to review my notes later and think things over.

Selection

Go through the evaluation sheets and the notes you made on the interview question sheets for each candidate. Rule out candidates who cannot meet all of your requirements as far as hours are concerned or did not reach the standard score you have set on the tests. Rule them out even if you liked them on a personal level. You will not do them or yourself a favor by hiring them for a job that does not suit their abilities or fit their schedule.

If you are lucky enough to be left with more than one applicant who displayed the skills and qualities that you require, there are other factors you can consider before making your final choice. If the community you serve has a sizable population of immigrants, for example, your library will already be making efforts to meet their needs by stocking materials in languages other than English and by spreading the word about the free services and many other benefits that come with registering for a library card. If one of your suitably qualified candidates is from a local ethnic community, hiring that person will fit in with the existing library policy of reaching out. Taking on someone from a diverse background can have other positive effects too. Some of the newcomers to our country have little in the way of education and are often wary of any institution that they think is linked to the government, including the library. Yet they want to help themselves and do what is best for their children. Seeing someone in the library with their own background and being able to approach that person for basic help and information will make them feel welcome in the library.

It is always difficult to choose between two well-qualified people. No one likes to turn a good candidate away, and it's important to be at peace with your decisions. If you know you are properly taking the needs of the library and the community into account, you are doing your job responsibly. If you don't feel confident about making these decisions at first, there is nothing wrong with asking a more senior staff member to help you.

When you have decided which candidate to hire, call this person and ask one more time if the hours you discussed are still convenient. Be very specific, because the candidate may have not completely understood what you said at the interview or her circumstances may have changed since the interview. Nothing is more annoying than to hire someone for a weekday afternoon slot and then have the shelver say a few days later that she can work only in the mornings. If you are both in agreement about the work hours, offer the position. It's best to make the offer by phone first. That way you will find out at once if the candidate has taken another job or is no longer interested, and you will not waste time and postage sending an offer by mail.

If you would have been happy to hire a different candidate in this round of hiring, let this person know that you will be in touch for a further interview if another position opens up within the next six months. The purpose of a second brief interview is to give him a reminder of the requirements of the job and to come to a clear understanding about the days and hours you require him to work. If you are in agreement, then you make an offer on the spot since you gave his application your full consideration the first time around.

Always let the people you are not interested in hiring know the outcome of their interviews. Write rather than call to avoid being drawn into any awkward discussion of your reasons for declining to hire them. Using regular mail rather than e-mail will also discourage any ongoing dialogue. In addition, a letter indicates that you have taken time and trouble over your decision. They will be pleased that you did and will be unlikely to harbor any resentment. If an unsuccessful candidate contacts you by phone to ask if you are going to offer her a job before you have had a chance to send out your "no thank you" letters, you can say that you are still in the process of interviewing and deciding and assure her that she will hear from you whatever the outcome. I have included sample letters for these situations in the appendix.

If you take a methodical approach to each interview and make consistent use of evaluation tools and tests, you will greatly improve your chances of hiring people who will quickly become efficient shelvers and reliable employees.

CHAPTER THREE

TRAINING

The time you invest in training new staff will benefit everyone. It will give shelvers the knowledge and confidence to do their jobs well, and if they are working efficiently, then the public and other library staff will be able to find the materials they need without annoying delays. Moreover, your own working life will be much more pleasant if you are not constantly dealing with complaints about misplaced items and slow restocking.

It is important to help new shelvers realize that they have a vital role to play in the day-to-day life of the library if you want them to take pride in their work.

Begin by taking your newly appointed pages on a tour of the building. Start with the basics, such as which entrance they are to use, where they are expected to park their car, and how they can secure their personal belongings during working hours. They will also need to know where they can take a break and the locations of staff restrooms. Then you can begin to teach them how the library functions. Explain the process that each item goes through as it is checked out and then checked back in. Take them behind the scenes and show them where newly acquired items are cataloged, labeled, and issued with bar codes. Walk through the public areas and point out all the services that the library offers. Stop by the circulation and reference desks and all the other departments and introduce the new shelvers to the others who work at the library. This gives your coworkers a chance to make the newcomers feel welcome.

When a patron goes into the catalog, finds that the library owns the item she wants, and that it is checked in, she is well on the way to being satisfied. If the item then turns out to be exactly where the computer said it would be, she is likely to be very pleased. You can tell your new shelvers that their mission is to make sure that as many patrons as possible have the satisfaction of finding that the materials they want are in the right place.

During the first session on the job, some time will need to be spent filling out tax forms and reviewing the job description. (The appendix contains an example of a page job description.) You will also need to make photocopies of personal identification documents. Be sure to have a folder ready in advance, with all the necessary items in it. This will show your newcomers that you have thought about their arrival ahead of time and that you are ready to help them settle in and get started. This is especially important if you are dealing with young people who have not held a job before. You want to dispel any anxiety so they can concentrate on the task at hand. If possible, take new shelvers to a quiet area where you can both sit down while you explain the various forms to them. This is also a good opportunity to go over the hours that you are expecting your newly hired shelvers to work. I strongly advise that you do this even though you have explained it twice already (once at the interview and once when you made the job offer). I have known shelvers who were hired on the clear understanding that they would be working during the afternoons on Mondays, Tuesdays, and Thursdays and who arrived for their first shift to give me the news that they would be available only on Wednesday and Friday mornings. If you find yourself in a similar situation, don't feel that you have to go through with the hiring process. Just tell your recently hired person that you are sorry but your offer is conditional on his being able to work the hours that you require and that if he cannot meet this condition, you will have to look for someone who can. I suggest that you do this even when you may be short of staff. It makes little sense to hire someone who has already demonstrated that he can't, or won't, listen to what you say.

New library employees are expected to absorb huge amounts of information, and it's important to let them know from the outset that you welcome their questions. You don't want anyone to put materials in the wrong place because they are too nervous or embarrassed to seek guidance. When they do come looking for help, be sure to say something like, "Good question" or "I'm glad you asked." Remember that being open to questions is a great way of finding out whether you are explaining tasks clearly. Use this feedback to help you find better ways of sharing your knowledge. I always used to tell my new recruits that I would be worried if they *didn't* keep asking me questions. Once the tour is over and the paperwork is complete, I suggest that you let your new shelver tackle a cart of books right away.

SHELVING

You need to be sure that a new page can shelve accurately but don't want to make her uncomfortable by constantly looking over her shoulder as she puts her first cart of books away. It's also true that you have better things to do with your valuable time. The answer to this conundrum is to use training slips. These are brightly colored pieces of paper the size of a bookmark with your library logo and "Training Slip" printed on them. They should also display a message for patrons, letting them know that it is okay to check out a book that has a training slip in it. (The appendix contains a sample training slip.)

Start the process by asking your new employee to put a cart of books in order in the sorting area. Have her tuck a training slip inside each book at the same time, leaving a third of the slip sticking out at the top. It's important to be positive and encouraging from the beginning, so when you introduce the concept of the training slips, avoid putting a negative slant on it. Telling someone who has been in the building for only an hour that using these slips is going to help you find all her mistakes strikes entirely the wrong note. It's far better to say that the training slips will show you at once how well she is doing and will give you both a chance to talk about anything that needs clarification. Once your trainee has the cart ready, check that everything is in order and have her correct any errors before you head out to the stacks. Give some thought to the way you draw attention to these errors. Remember that your aim should be to boost confidence, so I recommend that you *never* use any variations of the following:

"I can see three mistakes on this cart already."

"You're not being very careful, are you?"

"You did much better than this on your test."

Remarks like these make people feel as if you regard them as idiots—certainly no way to begin a working relationship. It's much better to let your trainee know that she is experiencing a learning curve that is absolutely normal. So you could instead say:

"Some of these long Dewey numbers can be very confusing."

"This one catches everyone out at first."

"It looks as if you have nearly everything in the right place."

When you get to the stacks, be specific about how you want the job done. This is the time when you can lay the foundations of efficient working habits. It's a good idea to shelve the first few books yourself. As you do so, you can talk about and illustrate the following guidelines:

- Park your cart across the end of the book stack, leaving the aisle clear for patrons.
- Check the books on either side of each one that you shelve in case there is an error in the sequence.
- Reshelve any books that you find out of order.
- Be especially careful at the ends and beginnings of shelves so that the correct sequence of materials is not interrupted or confused.
- Concentrate on accuracy.
- Straighten up the books on the shelf as you go, and pull the books forward to the shelf edge.
- Push bookends into place.

- Shift books to the next, or the previous, shelf if they are overcrowded.
- Pick up and reshelve any books that have been left lying on the floor or piled up at the ends of the shelves.
- Bring any damaged or wrongly labeled items you find back to the sorting area.

Ask your new page to leave the books she shelves sticking out a couple of inches so that you can spot them easily later.

It is also a good idea to let your trainee know that patrons are allowed to touch, and even walk away with, the materials that she has just put away. I neglected to do this once and came back to find my new shelver and a member of the public in the middle of a rather tense standoff. Also stress that if a patron asks her a question, she should reply that she is a brand-new employee and direct the patron to staff at the nearest public desk. Finally, tell her that since she did so well on her tests, you are sure she will do a splendid job. And then go away and leave her to her work.

After half an hour or so, check on her progress. It's not unusual to find that she has made half a dozen errors. People often don't realize at first just how careful they have to be with Dewey numbers, especially the long ones, or they don't know that a group of fiction books written by the same author should be further alphabetized by title. When you find an error, draw the trainee's attention to the book in question and ask her if she notices anything about it. Often trainees see at once where they went wrong and can then have the satisfaction of putting things right themselves. If they don't understand why a book is in the wrong place, point out where the error lies and then ask them to try again. Be patient and stay calm. If the neophyte shelver is really struggling with an item, just show her where it goes. Be sure to draw attention to the fact that she has managed to shelve most of the cart accurately. In my experience, new employees get past these small hiccups very quickly, and they are not worth dwelling on. You can expect the next cart to still have one or two errors, but the third cart will usually have none. Some people take a little longer to get to the point where they are error free, so from time to time, you may need to use the training slips for up to the first half-dozen carts. And then the training slips can be put away.

Occasionally you may come across an employee who, in spite of all your guidance, does not reach the standard of accuracy you are looking for. I once hired someone who made six to eight errors on each of his first three carts. This was a new experience for me, but I was prepared to go on working with him. The next time he came to work, I used the training slips again, and the error rate remained steady for the next three carts. I took the person to one side and asked him how he thought he was doing. He was under the impression that he was doing splendidly. At this point, I could not see a way forward and had to explain that I could not spare the time to check every book he shelved and would have to let him go. If you find yourself in a similar position, be polite and as kind as you can, but be firm.

You can't afford to keep a chronic error maker on your team. And, yes, this shelver had passed the tests at the interview stage.

I never told my new pages that I expected them to have a cart of books shelved within a certain amount of time. I was always far more concerned with accuracy. If you give your employees the time and space to establish good shelving skills, they usually pick up speed naturally.

Each time that you introduce a trainee to a new duty, make sure that you explain and demonstrate exactly what is required. If you get into a habit of doing this, it should help your new staff acquire competence at an encouraging pace. Of course there will be times when you think you have shown someone all she needs to know about a task, only to come back later and find her going about it entirely the wrong way. When that happens, try to avoid any displays of annoyance. If you embarrass or humiliate a trainee, she is much less likely to be receptive to any further instructions that you give her. It's best to accept right away that her lack of understanding could be your fault. A useful phrase in circumstances like this is, "It looks as if I didn't explain this very clearly. What I would like you to do is . . ." I always found that this approach worked very well and that my staff respected me for being prepared to admit that I could be at fault.

It's important to remember that the areas where materials are checked in and sorted can look completely chaotic to a newcomer. Do not expect new pages to immediately know the difference between carts that contain checked-in items, which can be taken away and shelved, and carts that contain unchecked items. If you do not have a system in place where each cart is clearly marked with brightly colored labels I strongly suggest that you set one up.

You need your employees to turn up on time, get busy, and stay busy in order to cope with the constant flow of returned materials. It's best to be clear about your expectations from the beginning. If breaks are meant to be fifteen minutes long, you need to make that plain on the first day and follow up with instant reminders if you notice anyone taking longer. And of course you will get far more cooperation in this matter if you are back from your own breaks on time. It also does no harm to point out from the first day that breaks should be taken in the middle of a shift and may not be saved until the end in order to leave work early.

Shelvers are always going to spend a high proportion of their time working alone in the stacks, and it is worth making it clear from the start that the library expects them to avoid the following distractions:

- Friends and family members who are visiting the library should certainly be greeted, but long conversations must be politely discouraged or postponed until break time or the end of a shift.

- Shelvers should be encouraged to acknowledge patrons in a friendly manner and give them appropriate assistance but should avoid being drawn into long social chats.

- In the course of their work, shelvers inevitably come across all manner of interesting and absorbing books. They must understand that they cannot take time out to browse or read them. They can check them out and take them home instead.

- If another shelver is working a couple of stacks over, shelvers may find it tempting to stop what they are doing and socialize. This not only wastes time but gives the appearance of wasting time to any nearby patrons.

When you are making points like these, it's helpful to avoid phrases that begin with "Don't." People are generally more receptive to instructions that are given in a positive way. Even if you are giving what amounts to a command, you can bookend it with remarks that will make it sound more like a suggestion—for example:

- "You'll probably come across a lot of books that interest you when you shelve, and there just isn't time to stop and read them, but please feel free to check out whatever you'd like to enjoy later."

- "We all enjoy seeing our friends when they come here, but of course we have to remind them they'll have to wait until we have finished working if they want to talk to us for any length of time."

Occasionally I have had new shelvers ask me if they could listen to music while they work. My answer was always no, for the following reasons.

- If your ears are blocked by headphones, you may not hear a patron who is trying to ask for assistance.

- Patrons may not feel they can approach you at all if they see the headphones.

- If you are in a quiet area by yourself, you should be aware of who else is around for safety reasons.

- You should be giving your work your full attention.

I did not allow the use of cell phones during work periods. People were free to make all the calls they liked during their breaks, as long as they did not disturb other staff members.

Any time that you are about to tell people what to do, try to imagine how you would like to be given the same instructions yourself. If you treat your employees with courtesy and are patient and good humored, they will be more inclined to give you their full attention and their best efforts.

All shelvers spend a lot of time pushing heavy carts around a building that is populated by other staff members and by patrons. Always assume that the following advice to trainees is necessary:

- Never run with a cart under any circumstances.

- Always check the area around you carefully before moving off. Small children can be hard to see if they are directly in front of your cart.

- Never let children ride on your cart.
- Never attempt to ride on a cart yourself.
- Move slowly across the ends of the aisles. Patrons can emerge from them very suddenly.
- Never try to squeeze you and your cart onto an elevator if it is already full of patrons.
- Let patrons with wheelchairs or strollers go ahead of you and, if necessary, instead of you.
- Steer your cart around the building as carefully as you can. Make an effort to avoid collisions with walls, library furniture, elevator doors, and so forth.

Some of these instructions are obviously aimed at younger and more high-spirited trainees who might be tempted to take part in a cart race or to sit on an empty cart while riding in an elevator. It can be surprising, though, how careless even some mature adults can be about scraping inanimate objects or crashing into them, so I recommend that you give all new employees some book cart "driver's ed."

AUDIOVISUAL MATERIALS

I suggest that you wait until new trainees are comfortable with their ability to put away printed materials correctly before you introduce them to the array of audiovisual (AV) formats that you are likely to have in your library. In my experience, these items call for a more experienced level of sorting and ordering skills simply because many of them look so similar. Books are all the same format too, but it is not difficult to tell the difference between, say, a picture book and a young adult novel. In fact, you could probably do it with your eyes closed, going just by size and weight.

By contrast, my library's DVDs are all presented in the same-size packaging and security cases but can be found in the different collections.

Movies (over 10,000 of them) are divided into multiple genres:

- Action
- Drama
- Family Friendly/Children
- Fantasy/Science Fiction
- Foreign Language with English subtitles
- Horror/Mystery

There are also hundreds of DVDs with other designations such as these:

- TV series
- Kids' DVDs

- Youth nonfiction
- Anime
- Opera
- Spanish Youth
- Spanish Adult
- Russian language
- Polish language
- English as a second language
- Adult nonfiction
- Juvenile nonfiction

This means that anyone attempting to shelve a DVD correctly has to decide which of eighteen possible locations it should go to. In addition, our library has four kinds of video games that also look exactly like DVDs. To ensure that all of these end up in the right places, we use different colors for call number labels, and the various movie genres all have a colored identifying dot on the spine. It is entirely understandable that any newcomer could be mightily confused by all this.

It's a good idea to let trainees get used to handling these items one section at a time rather than just giving them a whirlwind tour of all the AV items you carry. If you immerse someone in the movies for a couple of shifts, he will have a chance to thoroughly absorb everything he needs to know about the genres. Begin by having him do some sorting behind the scenes before you send him out to shelve the movies. That way you can spot if he is having any trouble with distinguishing one colored label or dot from another before any damage is done.

Even if your new employee has been with you a week or two and is shaping up nicely by the time you introduce him to the AV materials, I recommend that you continue escorting him personally to any section that he has not worked in before. You should still be taking every opportunity to explain exactly where things go and how you want the work done. If you demonstrate that it matters to you that everything gets put away in the right place, then the people who work for you are more likely to care as well.

The music collection in a medium-sized library also offers many chances for items to stray from their proper homes. Most CDs come in the same size package, but in any library a collection of them is likely to be split among multiple classifications. The broad areas, such as classical, popular, rock, and children's music, can be subdivided into many smaller sections. My library has fifty-eight such divisions.

If you have an area where you presort music CDs, have your trainee start there. The artwork on the cases may give some clues as to genre, but it will soon be apparent to anyone trying to differentiate between one CD and another that the only information that really counts is on the label.

FIGURE 3.1   *CD SPINE LABEL*

CD
MR
LINK
HT
L-52

Unlike the straightforward spine labels found on books, which rarely go beyond two lines, the ones on CDs may have as many as five lines, and the information on them is probably abbreviated. For instance, in my library, the label that would appear on a CD called *Hard Times* by the band Linked Arms is shown in figure 3.1. The first line identifies the type of item it is. The second line tells us that the classification is MR, denoting rock music. LINK is the first four letters of the band's name. HT are the initial letters of the album's title. L-52 gives the first letter of the band's name plus the last two digits of the recording company's identifying number for this item. Shelving this CD with any degree of accuracy requires paying attention to the middle three lines on the label. The shelver should arrive at the correct section, then the band's location among the other artists beginning with L, and the CD's place within the other recordings, if any, by Linked Arms.

All of this needs to be spelled out precisely to trainees. Never assume that anything about the way your library classifies and labels its materials is self-explanatory to a newcomer.

Once again I advise immersion as the best way of familiarizing some-one with materials of this kind. Take a walk around the CD display units with your trainee and point out the variety of music that is on offer. You could also talk about the broad spectrum of musical tastes that your patrons are likely to show and how they all want to be able to find their favorite artists and albums with a minimum of frustration. I then have trainees sort and shelve in one area at a time. Someone who is not familiar with classical music, for instance, may need a little time to grasp the difference between the symphonies and the concertos, not to mention the instrumental solo sections. And a trainee who has not previously paid much attention to popular music may have trouble at first in distinguishing among the many and varied compilation albums that tend to populate that area.

Audiobooks may be less confusing to handle than some other AV mate-rials since they are usually labeled in a similar way to printed books and fall into the same categories and genres. Nevertheless, there are still likely to be things you need to spell out to trainees. For instance, it may be that juvenile audiobooks get shelved together with their printed cousins but adult audiobooks are housed as a separate collection. Are adult books on CD shelved apart from those on cassette, or do they all go together? You can't assume that any of this is going to be obvious, even to someone who has been training with you for a week or two.

In addition to these formats, libraries are likely to offer a wide variety of AV items, ranging from back issues of magazines on microfilm to computer software to digital audiobooks. My recommendation is to introduce trainees to all of these formats and provide detailed instruction rather than just assuming that their general aptitude for shelving will be enough. Even if you intend to have a new trainee work mainly with printed materials, introduce them to all collections in the library. You never know when sickness or a shortage of staff will make it necessary for your shelvers to help out in sections they don't normally handle.

SHELF READING

The task of shelf reading soon grows tedious and requires a great deal of concentration. I always found it necessary to be very specific about how I wanted it done. It is also essential to explain to a newcomer why shelf reading needs to be done at all:

- Books are often put back in the wrong place in heavily browsed areas.
- Shelf reading gives us a chance to find books that are damaged, require cleaning, or are in the wrong section.
- Areas that are tidy and in good order are more attractive to patrons.
- Shelf reading fits in with the overall goal of keeping library materials properly organized and findable.

Take your trainees to the shelves and demonstrate *exactly* how you want the job done, and make no apologies for being particular. Tell them, for example,

"Touch each book as you read its spine label. If you use only your eyes, it's too easy to skip items."

"Pull the book if it is dirty, damaged, needs a new label, or is in the wrong place."

"Tidy up as you go along. Move books to the left and push in bookends."

"Don't shelf-read for longer than thirty minutes. Your eyes and brain will have had enough by then."

"Record your progress in the shelf reading log."

The grandly titled "shelf reading log" can be a binder with a page for each section. When someone heads out for the adult fiction or the juvenile 600s, she can take the sheet with her, note the date and the progress made, and then return the sheet to the binder.

It would be ideal if your pagers could do some shelf reading during each shift they work, but this will not always be possible at busy times. I used to require a minimum of thirty minutes per week and found that everyone could manage that. Remember that if you want to check on how a trainee (or an established staff member) performs this task, you must choose a time when he is still working on a section. Even if you arrive as early as five minutes after someone has finished shelf reading, you will have no way of knowing whether she is responsible for any out-of-place items. I used to assign people to shelf-read the same sections that they regularly worked in. Familiarity with materials in an area makes it easier to spot items that are out of place. I also found that giving someone the overall responsibility for an area encouraged him to take pride in keeping it in good order.

SHIFTING

Library collections are not static. New materials are constantly being added and old items weeded out. In order to keep the materials evenly spaced on the shelves, your staff need to shift constantly. If they do not, you will soon end up with some shelves jam-packed and others almost empty. This looks untidy and unprofessional and should be avoided as much as possible. Also, patrons have difficulty browsing through tightly packed shelves. If they have to wrestle a book out of its slot just to take a look at it, they will be disinclined to waste their time trying to wedge it back in if they decide not to take it. As a result, more books will be left lying about on the floor or other shelves. Another disadvantage of allowing things to get to this stage is that the shifting process then becomes even more time-consuming and tedious, and pages may go out of their way to avoid doing it at all.

It's important to emphasize the need for regular shifting in the early stages of instruction, but I usually waited until the training slips had been dispensed with before getting into detail. Here are some points you can bring up when you are telling someone that you expect him to pay regular attention to this aspect of shelving:

- Aim to leave the right-hand third of each shelf as free space.
- Overcrowded shelves will make your work slow and difficult.
- Crowded books are not pleasant to browse.
- If you come across an area that needs adjustment while you are shelving, tackle it right away.

- If you don't fix it at once, a two-minute job can quickly grow into a problem that will consume thirty minutes or more of your time.
- If you skip this task, there is no way to hide it!

Once in a while, there will be a need to do some large-scale shifting. This can happen if the weeding of a particular area within a section is not keeping pace with the number of new items being added to it. Shelving can become difficult, if not impossible, in such areas even with the best efforts of your staff. Under these circumstances, I suggest that you assign a number of people to undertake a major shift all at one time. In this way, the job doesn't become a huge burden for one individual.

I recommend that you walk around the stacks at regular intervals so that you can spot potential shifting problems before they have a chance to get out of hand. Tidy and evenly filled shelves are pleasing to the eye and speak of a well-run organization. Encourage your staff to take pride in them.

CLOSING PROCEDURES

My experience is that what shelvers do, or don't do, at closing time is one of the topics most likely to bring you complaints from other departments. In order to keep your customers satisfied, it's best to know exactly what they want. If you don't already have checklists for the tasks that need to be completed at closing time, I suggest that you speak to your colleagues who work at the public inquiry desks. Using their thoughts and your own ideas, you should not have difficulty coming up with a procedure you can all agree on. Once you have that clear, you will be in a position to instruct your staff on how to do a thorough job. The training needed is going to be a bit more involved than just telling someone to go to an area and tidy up for an hour.

Figure 3.2 shows cleanup checklists that you can use as examples. As these lists show, a lot of work needs to be done at the end of the library day, and most of it requires an eye for detail. In my view, you have to walk a new employee through this process at least once, and preferably two or three times. I found it useful to stress the following points:

- Always speak to the staff at the public desks first. They can tell you if there has been unusual or heavy traffic in any areas.
- Keep an eye on the clock. That way you won't get absorbed by a single task and have no time left for the rest.
- Try to notice when individual patrons are leaving so you can tidy up after them.
- If there isn't enough time to do everything, you can put items that need reshelving on an orphan cart and take it back to the sorting area.
- If two or three shelvers are cleaning up on one floor, you should be working in different sections so that everything gets covered.

FIGURE 3.2 *CLOSING TIME PROCEDURES* `WEB`

First Floor Closing Time Procedure

- Let the staff at the public information desks know you will be cleaning up. Ask if there are any areas that need urgent attention.
- Pick up any stray materials on the floor or piled on shelves and put them away as time permits. Items that have not been reshelved by closing time can go on the orphan cart.
- Straighten materials on shelves by pushing in bookends.
- Reshelve all reference items IMMEDIATELY. Do not put them on orphan carts.

Picture Book Area

- Check the toys, puzzles, and puppets. Reassemble anything that needs it and put away in appropriate bins.
- Tidy the play area. Put away noncirculating stuffed animals, cardboard books, toys, and puppets.
- Tidy the puzzle table. Return all assembled puzzles to the rack. Push in chairs.
- Scan shelves for books that are upside down, inside out, or out of place. This is especially important in the Picture Book area, which is always heavily browsed.

Teen Zone

- Put magazines away, clear tables, and push chairs in.
- Put YA materials in order, if needed.

AV

- Push all CDs and DVDs back against their dividers.
- Reshelve any stray materials on floor or on wrong shelves.

Checkout Area

- Do not turn off any of the catalog computers or the copiers.
- Check for any stray materials left by the copier, catalog computers, and self-checkout stations.
- Check with staff at the public information desks when you are finished and bring full orphan carts back to the circulation area. Replace with empty carts.
- Pick up all trash from floor, tables, shelves, and anywhere else.
- Clear off study tables and push in chairs.
- Do a final check for any stray items you missed.

FIGURE 3.2   *CLOSING TIME PROCEDURES (CONT.)*

Second Floor Closing Time Procedure

- Let the reference desk staff know you are there to clean up. Ask if any areas need immediate attention.
- Check the silent study room for library materials and return the items to where they belong. Turn out the lights if the room is empty. If it's still occupied, mention it at the reference desk and remember to check back later.
- Put away all current magazines and newspapers and tidy the seating area.
- Check all tables and study carrels for books and other materials. Reshelve as much as you can; then put the rest on an orphan cart.
- Push all chairs up to the tables.
- Pick up all scrap paper, pencils, and trash. Pencils go in cups by catalog computers. There is a box for clean scrap paper at the reference desk. Dispose of trash properly.
- Return all back issue magazines and newspapers to the stack area. Shelve if time allows, or place them on the sorting cart.
- Straighten the business reference and consumer reference areas.
- Check ALL aisles for stray materials left on the floor or piled on shelves. Reshelve as much as possible or put them on an orphan cart.
- Push in bookends and refill empty display easels.
- Reshelve items that have been left on the small carts at the ends of aisles.
- Reshelve reference materials. Please put a red dot on any item that does not have one (for usage survey).
- Put kick stools in the aisles where patrons can see them.
- Turn off microfiche machines. Put any microfilm in the orange box on top of the microfiche cabinet.
- Replenish small scrap paper at all public computer terminals.
- CHECK BACK AT THE DESK TO SEE IF ANYTHING ELSE NEEDS TO BE DONE.

- Remember that the staff and patrons who come in when the library opens the next morning will immediately notice how well you have cleaned up.

When you have taken your new employee through this routine yourself, try to team her up with a more experienced page the next few times until you are sure she has a thorough grasp of what needs to be done.

It's a good idea to keep as close an eye as you can on the way all of your shelvers, new and old, perform their closing duties. Usually the first thing they tend to disregard is the need to report to the reference desk before and after tidying up. The people at the desk are usually busy at this time themselves and may not realize that the shelvers are skipping this work until it has been going on for a few days. It's not unusual for shelvers to start going about in pairs during the cleanup period so they can chat with each other rather than splitting up to tackle separate parts of the floor. And sometimes your staff develop the habit of going back to base ten minutes before closing time in order to fill out their time sheets or put their coats on. How can you prevent this downward slide?

- Talk to the reference staff and ask them to let you know at once if they are not happy with what the pages are doing at closing time.
- Leave copies of the closing-time procedure checklists at each reference desk.
- Take a tour of the library at closing time every couple of weeks even if you have not received complaints.
- Compliment anyone you find doing a particularly good job of the closing routine.
- If you arrive first thing in the morning, take a good look around. If tasks have been missed, write a note in the log of the shelvers concerned or speak to them at the first opportunity.

Once your pages know that you are going to be checking this aspect of their work on a regular basis, they will be less inclined to let things slide.

MISCELLANEOUS TASKS

It's likely that in almost every library, those who are given the title of "shelver" will be also be expected to perform a variety of other tasks. Your job is to see that the people who work for you are competent in all that they do. Don't be tempted to take shortcuts. If you are asking your new trainees to contents-check returned AV materials for the first time, go through the process with them step by step. It can be a tedious job, but there is a purpose to it. Missing or damaged DVDs or CDs need to be found and noted. In that way, they can be recovered from patrons or withdrawn so they don't become a source of annoyance for the next person unlucky enough to check them out. Always explain why something needs to be done. It's much more pleasant and rewarding to do work that you know is of benefit to someone else.

It is worth taking the trouble to show a new page the right way of going about even a job as simple as emptying the parking lot book drop.

There are things that may never occur to some people if you just give them a wheeled bin and the key and send them outside to get busy. Here are a few of the points you might want to draw attention to:

- Avoid collisions with walls and library furniture on the way in and out of the library.
- Give way to patrons.
- Be very careful to avoid hitting any security system sensors at the main doors.
- Park the empty bin securely while opening the drop-off container.
- Pull the filled bin out of the drop box gently to avoid dislodging loose materials.
- Rearrange materials so that they do not slide off the top.
- Search the floor of the bin for fallen items.
- Park the filled bin carefully so that it does not run into a car while you are putting the empty one in place.
- Lock the door!
- Don't hurry with the filled bin. It's heavier and harder to control than the empty one.
- Put the key back!

I strongly recommend that any keys that have to be available to all of your staff have a large object such as a twelve-inch ruler as part of their key chain. It is too easy to put an unencumbered key in your pocket and go home with it.

As you can see, the instructions for changing a drop-off bin are simple enough, maybe even blindingly obvious, but the whole process will go much more smoothly if trainees are made aware of them from the start.

SHELVERS DON'T DO REFERENCE!

Anyone who works in a library knows, or should know, that shelvers are not paid to answer reference questions. Nevertheless, members of the public often think that the person putting the books away in the law section is just the one to help them with their question about beating their traffic ticket or suing their condo board. It's not enough to say to new shelvers, "Oh, and by the way, don't answer any reference questions." That doesn't help them very much, and it won't do your patrons a lot of good either. We all need to recognize that these encounters in the stacks are an opportunity to guide patrons to the service point they were reluctant to approach in the first place: the reference desk. Giving your staff a few phrases that they can use in this situation will help to reinforce the idea that you want them to take specific action:

"The people at the reference desk can help you with that. It's this way."

"If you come over to the reference desk, I'm sure they will be able to find you some information."

"Would you like to follow me to the reference desk? They will be happy to help you with that."

"Let me take you to our experts."

I strongly suggest that you encourage shelvers to walk the patron over to the desk and hand him or her off to the staff there. If the patron declines to go, then I suggest that the shelver visit the desk staff anyway to let them know that a patron may need help but seems unwilling to ask for it.

When you equip your staff with verbal tools like this, a number of things are achieved:

- Shelvers can quickly and politely get out of a situation they are not equipped to deal with.
- The patron does not waste time explaining his needs at length to someone who cannot help him.
- The reference staff gets the chance to meet the needs of the patron.
- The patron will be favorably impressed by the helpful behavior of your shelver.
- The shelver will be able to take pride in having dealt with the situation in a competent way.

I have often had my staff ask me, "But what if a patron asks me something that I know about? Why can't I give them an answer?" In the face of such a question, it can be helpful to let your trainees know that even the staff working at the reference desks are not allowed to give answers off the top of their heads. They must check and cite their sources, even if they are doing something as simple as spelling a word they are already familiar with. The more you can tell your shelvers about how much is involved in even a straightforward reference interview, the better they will realize that it's not something they should be attempting.

You can take an example such as a patron approaching a shelver with a piece of paper in hand and asking "Can you show me where this book is?" That sounds like the beginning of a simple transaction in which the shelver looks at the information and uses his knowledge of the collection to lead the patron to the right shelf. But as we know, things are likely to be a good deal more complicated:

- Does the patron know if the library owns the book?
- Is it fiction or nonfiction, in print or in audio format?

- Are the title and author correct?
- If the patron looked up the item in the catalog, did she notice if it was checked in?
- Is this the book she really needs?
- Does the library have other books or materials that would be acceptable?
- Would an interlibrary loan be appropriate?

Once you make it clear to trainees the time and effort required to deal properly with situations like these, they will understand that patrons are much better off being helped by someone other than them. Their immediate response to the patron should be, "Did the catalog show that this book was on the shelf?" and if the answer is any variation on the theme of "no" or "I'm not sure," the shelver should redirect or escort the person to a reference desk.

Information is the business of the library, and every effort must be made to see that only accurate information is given out. Let your trainees know that they will be helping to maintain that high standard by following these procedures.

Although shelvers should not be answering reference questions, they can certainly be allowed to do the kind of informal readers' advisory that practically everyone in a library gets involved in sooner or later. If a shelver is working in the new fiction area and a patron picks up the latest best-selling suspense novel and asks for the shelver's opinion, she can give it if she has read the book. If your shelver then goes on to say that she also enjoyed another title very much, no harm is done. But if a patron approaches the shelver and asks for specific information about the publication dates of a series of books or suggestions about what to read next, the shelver must direct the patron to the readers' advisory or reference desk. The staff there will have a vast amount of information about books and authors and are practiced at asking questions that will help them match readers with books they are likely to enjoy or need to consult. I suggest that when you are giving a trainee the tour of the library, you introduce her to the people who handle your readers' advisory service and ask them to give your newcomer some idea of the resources they have available. In this way, trainees will understand that they will be doing patrons a favor by sending them to the right place to get help with their reading choices. It's always more effective to give someone a good reason for following instructions.

Shelvers can also be encouraged to be helpful to patrons by answering questions that are geographical, such as

"Where do I check out?"

"Where are the restrooms?"

"Where is the elevator?"

A question such as, "Where are the cookbooks?" falls halfway between reference and geography. A suitable answer is, "They are just over here in the 641s, but it's a big section and if you're looking for something specific, the people at the reference desk can help you find it."

Be sure to tell your staff that if a patron asks them a directional question and they are not absolutely sure of the answer, their response must be to walk the patron to the reference desk.

Computer access for patrons is almost universal in public libraries. The terminals are often placed in areas adjacent to the collections where shelvers are working, so their chances of being asked by someone to help them with searching the Internet or writing a document are quite high. Depending on how things are done in your building, you need to inform trainees of the limits that are in place regarding the amount and type of assistance they should give. For instance, it might be acceptable to show a patron how to change the line spacing in a document or find the job application section on a company website for them. These are simple tasks that take very little time. But what should a shelver do if a patron is asking for this type of help every two or three minutes? Most of us are willing to help others, and it's not hard to imagine a situation where someone who should be shelving could get sidetracked by a needy patron for a long time. This is another instance where you can give newcomers some guidance on how to extract themselves from such encounters and quickly return to their own work—for example:

"I'm sorry, I can't help you with that, but let me get someone who can."

"If you let them know at the reference desk you're having problems, they'll call someone from computer services to help you."

Public copiers give rise to similar encounters. There can be no objection to a shelver's stopping and quickly helping someone who is confused about where to put the money or how to select paper size, but anything more complicated is best left to others. The golden rule should always be never to waste the patron's time.

Because they are usually working in public areas, shelvers are perceived as being approachable and are sometimes the first to hear if a patron is dissatisfied with the library in some way. In these situations, shelvers should do more than offer sympathy. They should encourage the patron to take the complaint to someone who is in a position to deal with it. The key is to keep shelving staff well informed about library procedures for handling issues such as patrons' objecting to certain materials in the library's collections, complaints from the public about other patrons' behavior, or Internet viewing policies.

By keeping staff up to date with this kind of information, you enable them to steer miffed patrons in the right direction so that their questions and concerns can be handled speedily and sympathetically by the right people. It is also important that shelvers feel that they can approach reference staff or security staff if they come across any situation involving patron behavior that they think warrants intervention—for example:

- patrons who appear to need assistance (such as lost children)
- possible damage to library property
- theft of library property
- patrons leaving valuable items, such as laptop computers, unattended
- rowdy behavior
- viewing of pornography

It's clear that any time your library holds training sessions on the topics of patron behavior policy and safety issues, it makes sense for the pages and shelving staff to be included. If this is not happening, you might want to point out to your superiors that it is often the shelving staff who have first contact with patrons in the far-flung and hidden corners of the stacks. If they are fully informed about library services and policies, they can interact with those patrons in a helpful and meaningful way.

PERSONAL SAFETY

Libraries are widely seen as quiet havens from the noise and bustle of the outside world. There is some truth to this, but they are also public buildings and anyone is free to come in and make use of the facilities. It is essential to warn all new shelvers that they might find themselves on the receiving end of the unwanted attentions of a patron. The most obvious scenario might involve a young female employee shelving in a quiet part of the stacks late in the evening and being pestered by a male, but all shelving staff should be made aware of the possible dangers and they need to know that they are free to take any of the following actions if they feel threatened:

- telling the patron that the behavior is inappropriate
- alerting at least one other staff member to what is happening
- taking refuge immediately in a public area of the library
- shouting, "Get away from me!" very loudly
- calling the police

It's important to stress that no one must tolerate this type of nuisance. I suggest bringing the topic up from time to time at page meetings so that it is not forgotten. You could ask if anyone had a recent encounter with a patron that they would like to talk about. You could then lead a discussion about the incident and have staff suggest ways in which they might handle a similar situation.

TRAINING LOGS

I recommend keeping an individual training checklist for each page (see figure 3.3). This can be a sheet of paper listing the duties and collections that your pages need to be familiar with. It's a good idea to sit down with your new trainee at the end of his first few shifts and check off the areas

---

FIGURE 3.3 *TRAINING CHECKLIST LOG*   `WEB`

Name: _____

Date of Employment: _____

First Day
- ☐ employment/tax forms
- ☐ tour of library
- ☐ door codes
- ☐ scheduling procedures
- ☐ work logs

First Floor
- ☐ graphic novels/manga
- ☐ picture books
- ☐ cardboard books
- ☐ easy readers
- ☐ youth fiction
- ☐ paperbacks
- ☐ young adult
- ☐ youth new materials
- ☐ special collections
- ☐ comics/magazines
- ☐ movies/DVD
- ☐ movies/Blu-ray
- ☐ TV DVDs
- ☐ kid DVDs
- ☐ opera DVDs/videos
- ☐ youth audiobooks
- ☐ CDs

Second Floor
- ☐ adult fiction
- ☐ large print
- ☐ audiobooks
- ☐ adult paperbacks
- ☐ biography
- ☐ reference
- ☐ foreign language collections
- ☐ nonfiction
- ☐ high school area
- ☐ periodicals
- ☐ new titles

Other
- ☐ checking returned AV materials
- ☐ parking lot bin
- ☐ closing first floor
- ☐ closing second floor

---

that you both agree he has become proficient in. Pages can often feel over-whelmed by the sheer volume of detail that they have to absorb and like to be reassured that they are making progress. Keeping a written record is a good way of doing this.

At the top of this form, I always included the checklist of items to be covered on a page's first day. This served as a useful reminder to me and also helped to reinforce the idea that the new page and I were following an established procedure. I found that most new pages welcomed whatever structure I could give them, probably because they felt they were drowning in a sea of information.

If you are training more than one new employee at a time, this type of record is essential for keeping track of each individual's progress. I also used to meet with my established shelvers periodically to review what they were comfortable with and discuss any additional training needs. I had a staff of at least twenty to keep track of and used these records to make sure I didn't assign tasks to people who were not trained for them.

Training shelvers is time-consuming work, and to maintain high stan-dards of accuracy, you will have to repeat the painstaking process with everyone you hire. If you listen carefully to the questions that your train-ees ask, you will gain a valuable understanding of which aspects of their new job need the most explanation. By consistently making this kind of effort, you will be rewarded with employees who can be trusted to shelve accurately and carry out other tasks confidently and with a minimum of supervision.

A WORD ABOUT VOLUNTEERS

In the library where I work, we are lucky enough to have volunteers who do many useful things for us, but they never shelve. It would make no sense to insist on thorough training for our shelvers and then turn around and let any well-meaning member of the public come in and start putting books away. In my experience, a volunteer who expresses an interest in shelving is soon deterred by the thought of having to submit to any kind of train-ing. Volunteers are also not usually aware of the physical effort required for this work.

When I was in charge of the shelvers, I used volunteers for tasks that required little supervision. Although some were very good about turning up to help out at regular times, others just dropped in when they felt like it, and I preferred to give them work that did not require much supervision and could be done in my absence. I found that people enjoyed checking the contents of returned AV materials and putting movies in security cases and would come back week after week.

Some libraries have programs whereby members of the public or local organizations adopt a shelf or section and come in regularly to shelf-read and tidy up. If you like the sound of this, recommend it to the powers that be in your building. It could save some time for your staff.

If your library does allow volunteers to shelve or shelf-read, it is in your interest to insist that they take the same written and practical tests as potential employees. Any who do not meet the library's standards should be politely steered toward other activities. No other policy makes sense. If you are being held responsible for the good order of your library's collections, you must have a measure of control over the people shelving them, whoever they are.

CHAPTER FOUR

DAY-TO-DAY SUPERVISING

To some extent, you are always going to be training your staff. Library collections are fluid, and changes in location, labeling, or format can be frequent. On top of that is the unrelenting daily influx of returned materials. The need for clear and constant communication between you and your staff is vital. You want them to be willing to listen to you and respond quickly to any requests you make. The best and simplest way to achieve this kind of rapport is to pay attention to them:

- Greet them at the beginning of their shift whenever possible.
- Take an interest in anything they share with you regarding their life outside the library (within appropriate limits).
- Take a walk into the stacks when they are shelving, and ask them how they are getting on.
- Compliment them if their section is in good order.
- If you give someone a special task, make sure you thank her when she has completed it.

When you are going to congratulate someone on a job well done, try to do it as publicly as possible. We all like to be thanked, and we like other people to know that we have done well.

Pages are usually the lowest-paid workers in the building, and you are not likely to have much latitude when it comes to handing out pay increases. In most libraries, it's usual for everyone to be given a small cost-of-living raise of 2 or 3 percent a year. On top of that you will probably be allowed to make some further small discretionary amounts as merit increases. There is no point in agonizing over this. The minimum-wage situation is not of your making, and all of your employees are free to look for higher-paying work elsewhere. Let them know that you wish you could give them more, give the merit increases to your best workers, and then look for other ways to show your appreciation.

There are many small ways you can make your staff feel appreciated, and most of them don't cost much:

- Keep a supply of candy where your staff can help themselves.
- Celebrate birthdays with a card signed by as many staff as you can muster and some cookies.
- Have a "Star of the Week" board in a prominent place and post the names of shelvers who perform beyond expectations. A caution is that this works well only if you do it on a regular basis.
- Give a monthly prize to the shelver who finds the highest number of wrongly labeled items.
- Local businesses such as chain restaurants often donate coupons to libraries for staff use, and these can be handed out as rewards.
- If other departments say good things about your shelvers, make sure they all hear about it.

ALLOCATION OF DUTIES

Because the stream of returning materials never ends and must always be dealt with in a timely manner, it is not easy to give shelvers much choice in the work they must tackle. I have already said that I preferred to have my staff shelve specific areas on a regular basis. When one of your shelvers hands in his notice, you know you are in for yet another round of interviewing and training, but you will also have an opportunity to offer your remaining staff a chance to make some changes. This can be handled in a number of ways:

- You can offer the vacant section to your most senior page first and then keep going down the list until you find a taker.
- You can post the opening on the notice board to be filled on a first-come, first-served basis.
- You can invite everyone who would like to make a change to submit their names and then reallocate as you see fit.

Although it may seem to you that going from shelving adult fiction to putting picture books away won't make much of a difference, it may actually result in someone getting more enjoyment out of the workday. However you decide to handle it, the section you are left with can be taken up by your newly hired shelver.

SCHEDULING

I always tried to be as flexible as possible about scheduling as long as the needs of the library were being met. My daytime pages, who were mostly retirees or women with young children, usually had regular shifts that repeated on the same days each week, and it was not difficult to accommodate them. I used a computer program to create the basic monthly schedule. Once all the daytime shifts were set, I printed out a paper copy two weeks before the beginning of the month and pinned it up for the evening and weekend pages to look at. The longest-serving page would be allowed to choose shifts first and the most recent newcomer would be last. When signing up for shifts, they had to adhere to the following guidelines:

- You must work at least one Friday, Saturday, and Sunday per month.
- No shift may be longer than four hours.
- No one may work all weekend hours.
- No more than four days between shifts.
- Only five people can sign up for the same shift.
- There must be at least four pages on hand to close the library each night.

Software programs that allow multiple users to access the same schedule online are available, but there is a drawback to having your staff sit down at a library computer to work out their schedules. Most shelvers are part time and often work no more than four hours a day. If you allow them access to the Internet, the temptation to check their e-mail or social networking groups may be irresistible for some, and time will be wasted.

Because people had lives outside the library, there would be times when a shelver who had signed up for a shift would later find that it was going to clash with an important appointment or a family occasion. In those situations, I expected that person to organize a shift exchange with a coworker. I made it clear that I expected to get involved in looking for backups only if someone was taken ill suddenly and had no time to look for a replacement. Most pages were able to organize their working lives successfully, and by allowing them to do so, I spared myself a time-consuming task each month.

If any of my staff with young children asked to switch to evening hours when school was on vacation, I did my best to oblige. In the same way, I tried to accommodate any high school students who wanted some extra daytime hours in the summer. Because of the need for a full complement of staff at closing times, it was not always possible to let evening staff switch to earlier shifts, but as long as the library did not suffer, I was prepared to be flexible, and I suggest that you should be too. It is one of the few perks you can offer.

PAGE MEETINGS

I held page meetings every month and had a day session and an evening session so that as many people as possible could attend.

If you are supervising more than half a dozen pages, you will not have many opportunities to see them all at once, so it's important to make good use of these meetings. Prepare an agenda and both post it and distribute it so that everyone has a chance to think about the topics beforehand. Invite staff to add items to it. A typical agenda might contain the following items:

- welcoming new staff
- thanking any staff who are leaving for their efforts in the past
- information about new or changing collections
- changes in packaging or labeling
- errors that have been occurring frequently
- discussions of how to improve work flow
- upcoming training opportunities
- favorable comments from other departments
- agenda items suggested by shelvers

It was not unusual to have a list of eight to ten items that my staff needed to address each month. It was always helpful to have examples of the items in question at the meeting, but whenever you give people a list of ten things to remember all at once, they are not likely to retain more than a few for very long. Transforming the list into a quiz can work better. You can turn a recurring error into a multiple-choice question like this one:

- If a DVD has an orange spine label, where should it be shelved?
    a. Regular Movie Collection
    b. Adult Nonfiction
    c. Adult Foreign Language
    d. Youth Foreign Language

Allow everyone to mark their own papers, and don't collect them afterward. Your aim is not to humiliate anyone. You just want to remind them of a few things they should be aware of. Don't give the answers yourself, but invite the quiz takers to supply them. It's a chance for your staff to show how much they know, and it also gives them the opportunity to recognize gaps in their knowledge. Have some small edible prizes to hand out to those who do well on the quiz.

Always provide refreshments at your meetings or encourage people to bring some along. If the meetings are fun as well as informative, everyone benefits. A meeting is a rare chance for your shelvers to interact as a larger group and enjoy each other's company, and it is a good idea to encourage this aspect of your gatherings. If there is a day when you are not in the building and an unusually large buildup of materials has to be dealt with, you want your shelvers to cooperate to solve the problem. They are more likely to be willing to do so if they feel they are part of the same team.

Most of my pages worked twelve hours a week, but I also had two staff who were senior pages and worked twenty-one hours a week during daytime hours. I relied a great deal on these two people to keep things running smoothly and tended to set aside half an hour a week to meet with them and keep them as well informed as possible. I encouraged them to make suggestions about improving the way work was done, and I valued their input.

NOTICE BOARDS

There will be times in between monthly meetings when you will need to spread information to your staff. Pages often do not have easy access to e-mail or voice mail at work, and so a large and well-maintained notice board in a central location is an efficient tool. Work schedules and notices about any collection changes or additions should be posted here. (An example of a daily page work assignment schedule is in the appendix.) If a number of book drops need to be emptied on a regular basis, a list of times that this task must be done is useful.

If your library puts out daily lists of programs and events that are taking place in the building, put one up on your board too. Shelvers who are kept up to date will be ready to offer helpful information when people come into the library searching for the right meeting room. If another member of staff sends you a complimentary e-mail about the pages, always print it out and pin it on the board. Try to make the general layout of the notice board as attractive as possible. Make sure you get a copy of any posters about upcoming lunches or staff book discussion groups and pin them up too, so that your workers have the same opportunity as everyone else to be included in the social life of the library.

People who begin as pages or shelvers often go on to take up positions in other library departments. Put up information about any current in-house job openings. A good idea is to have a list of former pages and the posts that they went on to fill within the library world as encouragement to others to see where their current job might lead them.

PAGE MANUALS

Opinions vary about the usefulness of page manuals. I am in favor of them. You may not always be available to answer your employees' questions at the time they arise, and you are expecting them to absorb huge amounts of information. Having information compiled in a handy booklet can be useful. (See the example of the page manual in the appendix.)

I recommend that manuals contain some guidance on the following topics and anything else that you think is necessary:

- library phone numbers
- phone numbers of all pages

- scheduling procedure
- rates of pay and salary payment procedures
- dress code
- employee conduct guidelines
- review and assessment information
- a map of the library
- general notes on shelving fiction and nonfiction
- shelf reading guidelines
- cleanup routines
- specific information about the library's collections.

Give all new shelvers a copy of the manual and ask them to go through it at their leisure and then get back to you with any questions. They should keep their copy at home. Have a reference copy available to everyone at all times on your desk or some other central location.

I have included some excerpts from the page manual I used in the appendix.

WEB PAGES

Most libraries have staff information websites, and if you can arrange to have a copy of your page manual posted there, the computer-savvy members of your staff will make use of it. Make sure that they are aware of all the other information regarding employment rights and conditions that can be accessed using the website.

Supervising your team of shelvers is about communication and consistency. Make an effort to speak to every staff member each time you are in the building with them. Let them know exactly what you expect them to do. Keep them up to date with any changes that affect them. Listen to any suggestions they may have about how the work can be done more efficiently. Let them know when you and others are pleased with what they have done.

If you pay attention to them, they will pay attention to you.

CHAPTER FIVE

KEEPING YOUR SHELVERS IN GOOD ORDER

Sooner or later every supervisor has to confront an employee who is not doing her job as well as she should be, and tackling situations like this as early as possible is vital. If you let someone get away with performing poorly, you can be sure that the rest of the people you supervise will notice. Your best workers may start to wonder if there is any point to keeping up their own high standards. Others who might be inclined to slack off will see an opportunity to do just that.

If you are the only person in charge of the shelvers and the library is open seven days a week, it is obvious that you cannot be physically present for all that time. If you leave a group of younger pages to their own devices for the last shift of the day, you should not be too surprised if they spend more time talking than you would normally permit. It is a certainty that other library staff will notice these lapses and will not be slow to let you hear about them. The best way to keep situations like these down to a minimum is to get some help. I was able to count on the support of a member of our circulation department. I used to arrange most of my time away from the building to coincide with the times when she was scheduled to work. She was well placed to keep an eye on the shelvers and knew what they were supposed to be doing. We met weekly to review any problems, and she would leave me messages if anything needed more immediate attention. All of my shelvers were aware of this arrangement, and her deputy supervisor's duties were part of her job description.

When you have to speak to a shelver about behavior that is causing concern, be sure to do so in private. (No one likes to be reprimanded in public.) If you don't have an office of your own, borrow one or use a staff conference room for this meeting. In a calm and friendly tone of voice, ask the person in question to come with you. You can always suggest going over a training log or a daily log if you want to keep the reason for the meeting between yourselves. Once you are alone, begin by asking your page how he thinks he is doing. Ask him if he has any questions or concerns about the work he is being asked to do. Sometimes shelvers are aware they have a problem and are willing to talk about it, in which case it is not difficult to agree on a course of action.

When you are responsible for maintaining discipline among your staff, you must become familiar with the policies and procedures that your library has in place for dealing with these matters. Aim to deal as fairly and humanely as you can with your people within the library's guidelines.

Whenever you have a problem with a member of your staff and are not sure how to handle it, don't hesitate to seek advice. Talking to colleagues who also supervise others is useful. I have already mentioned how valuable it can be to have regular meetings with other shelving supervisors in your area. In the meetings of this sort that I went to, people often talked about difficult situations they had faced with their staff and how they had handled them. I didn't always agree with their way of doing things, but I welcomed the chance to hear their ideas

Here are some suggestions for dealing with specific problems.

NONAPPEARANCE FOR A SCHEDULED SHIFT

Failing to arrive for work without giving any advance warning is a serious matter, and you must never allow an instance of this behavior to pass without making inquiries. In some circumstances, this behavior can be excused:

- sudden illness
- a sudden family or personal crisis or bereavement
- involvement in an accident on the way to work
- being the victim of a crime
- any other event after which a person could not be reasonably expected to report for work or warn you about his or her absence

In a situation where no satisfactory explanation is given, you need to find out where the problem lies. Make contact with the person as soon as possible. If he does not provide a good enough reason for his absence, ask him to come in as soon as possible so you can have a talk with him. Let him know he will not be allowed to start another shift until this problem is resolved. When you are in a private setting, ask him if he is unhappy about any aspect of his job. Perhaps another staff member is making life difficult for him, and if this is the case, you need to know this. Help your employee understand that you are willing to work with him to resolve the problem, but make it clear that you have to know you can rely on him to show up when he is expected.

If you still don't get a satisfactory answer, I advise you to issue a written warning to your employee stating that another failure to turn up for a scheduled shift will result in dismissal. You have to be able to rely on your staff, and they must understand their obligations to you and to the library.

HABITUAL LATENESS OR POOR TIMEKEEPING

If you are going to tackle someone about this issue, you cannot simply come out with vague accusations. You must have the evidence at hand. A way to do this is to keep a record of this person's arrival and leaving times over at least a week. When you have evidence of a pattern, invite the page to meet with you. Begin the meeting by giving her a chance to open the discussion by asking her if she has any idea what you might want to talk about. When it seems appropriate, bring out your notes, and show her the list of the dates and times when she arrived late or was seen leaving early. If some of these lapses took place while you were not in the building, your employee may demand to know who told you about them. Never give out names. Simply say that your information comes from sources you trust; then move on. Remind her that by accepting a position as a shelver, she agreed to contract a set amount of her time to the library. Point out that her late arrival or early departure puts an unfair burden on her coworkers. Having reached agreement that there is a problem, you need to set out your requirements for solving it. If she cited traffic conditions as her reason for being late, suggest that she leave herself some extra time to make the commute to work. If it fits in with the needs of the library, you could offer her an alternative starting time while still requiring her to complete her allotted hours. Let her know that you will be monitoring her arrival and departure times closely for the next two weeks and that you expect to see an immediate and sustained improvement. Arrange to meet again at the end of that period to review the situation. It can be useful to make a record of these proceedings that you can both keep and refer to. A simple conduct agreement sheet is in the appendix.

This kind of intervention is usually enough, but if the problem persists, you need to make use of any further disciplinary procedures your library has in place, such as official warning letters. If that doesn't work, you may have to let this person go. You cannot afford to tolerate persistent lateness.

INAPPROPRIATE DRESS

Even if your library does not have a specific dress code, common sense dictates that safety and decency need to be taken into account when looking at clothing worn during working hours. Shelvers need to be comfortable and need to be able to stretch, bend, and crouch without restriction, but there is a balance to be kept between comfort and professionalism. You would be justified calling someone to account for a number of reasons, including these:

- showing cleavage of any sort when standing or bending
- revealing a bare midsection when standing, stretching, or bending
- displaying offensive wording on a garment

- wearing shorts if they are prohibited in your library
- wearing dirty or torn clothing
- having footwear that is too flimsy for safety

Since all your staff will be aware of any clothing policy in place at your library, you will be perfectly justified in asking anyone who is dressed inappropriately to go home and change before starting or continuing a shift. The time taken to go and fetch suitable clothing should not be paid for by the library. Since the experience is going to cost the offender money, it is unlikely to be repeated. I did make an exception once when a young shelver arrived in shorts for her first shift, and I realized I had forgotten to warn her beforehand that they were unacceptable. She was dismayed to find out that she was not properly dressed for work, but I explained that the fault was mine and allowed her to hurry back home and change on the library's time. It was a useful learning experience for both of us.

INAPPROPRIATE TALKING AND SOCIALIZING

Social exchanges at work are a good thing and should certainly be encouraged. If your coworkers greet you in a friendly fashion and ask how you are, you are likely to begin your day in an upbeat frame of mind and feel inclined to cooperate in whatever tasks you are given. As a supervisor, you will do well to try to sustain an atmosphere of goodwill, but if you notice that conversations about topics outside the library are taking up an excessive amount of time and hindering the flow of work, you need to take action at once.

Quite often all you need to do is politely break into the conversation and give all those involved some further instruction about what you would like them to be doing. There's no need to actually say that you want them to stop talking. Most people take the hint and get back to work. If someone is still inclined to keep chatting, you can set him a target that will leave no time for casual conversation—for example, "I'd really like to see you shelve three carts of adult fiction before we begin cleanup." You must be consistent. Once your shelvers know that any kind of chatfest is going to be noted and discouraged, they generally give up.

You will need to deal with those who persist in gabbing to excess on an individual basis. Speak to them in private and be calm and firm. Begin by explaining that their excessive talking is distracting to others and that you cannot ignore a behavior that is interfering with important tasks. Make sure they understand that behavior of this kind does not go over well with other library staff and that you are bound to hear about it even if you are not in the building at the time. You might also want to point out that it reflects poorly on them as individuals, the other shelvers, and you, their supervisor. Let them know that you expect to see an immediate improvement and that a failure to curb this behavior will lead to disciplinary action.

I often found it necessary to speak to individuals more than once about their excessive chatting but usually never had to take action beyond a second warning. Generally a person who is known to be a constantly long-winded talker will find coworkers gradually withdrawing from any but the shortest exchanges, mostly because they have better things to do with their time.

The most persistent group of talkers is likely to be younger school-age shelvers, especially if they work together in the evenings and on weekends. It's best to try and keep the problem from reaching the point where stern measures have to be taken. Some of your options might include

- Leaving them detailed instructions about the amount of work you expect to see completed. This might persuade them that they have no time to chat.

- Asking a staff member from another department to check in with your shelvers frequently to see how they are doing.

- Increasing your own evening and weekend hours so you can be on site to give more direct supervision.

Shelvers in this age group may also be inclined to take their enjoyment of socializing with each other so far as to begin taking their breaks all at the same time in the evenings. This is a bad idea on several levels:

- The larger the group, the longer the break is likely to be.

- Their joint absence will create a time period when no one is available to help other library staff with inquiries about returned and not-yet-shelved items.

- Such an obvious breach of good sense and discipline is bound to be noticed and cause annoyance on the part of other staff.

To combat this behavior, you need to have a rule in place that allows a maximum of two shelvers to go on break at the same time. All shelvers need to be aware of this regulation, and it does no harm to have it posted prominently in the work area. Alert other library staff and ask them to let you know if they see it being breached. Speak to any offenders as soon as possible after the event. Once people know they are being observed and that news of their transgressions will get straight back to you, generally their behavior improves.

I have known some supervisors who organize work so that the bulk of the shelving in their library is done during the day or even in the mornings before the library opens, and because of these arrangements, they employ only adults as shelvers. That is certainly one way of avoiding situations that can sometimes arise when teenagers are employed. But public libraries exist to serve their communities, and it can be argued that providing a number of young people with their first employment experiences is a worthwhile part of that service. This is something that has to be worked out by the board and staff of each library.

If you do employ high school students, you are bound to come across excess congregating and chatting sooner or later. When it happens, it will not necessarily be your young shelver's fault. It usually occurs soon after young people are hired. When you go into the stacks to see how they are getting along, you may find a trainee surrounded by half a dozen friends who have come into the library with the sole purpose of watching their buddy at work. It is important to act immediately. Be pleasant, but explain to them that their friend is operating on the library's dime and will not be free to meet with them until break time or the end of his shift. Then stand your ground. This is usually enough to persuade them to go and hang out elsewhere. They may come back another day, but if they get a similar reception, the novelty will wear off. The trainee is often embarrassed to have an audience anyway and will be relieved to see them go. If you encounter a group that will not give up, you can take them to one side and ask them if they want to be the reason that their friend loses a job. If that doesn't work, you may have to resort to excluding them from the building for a day or two until they get the point.

UNDERPERFORMANCE

If you have a shelver who has completed a few weeks of training and is not getting as much work done as you think she could, asking her to get a move on probably won't improve matters much. It's better to show her how the work is done. If you work alongside her for a whole shift and are able to demonstrate that you can easily shelve two carts to her one, you may make an impression that will yield results. This does not mean that you ask anyone to sacrifice accuracy for speed. What you will be doing is showing what can be achieved by concentrating on the task at hand.

It's also a good idea to pair one of your best workers with a shelver who needs to pick up the pace. You don't need to say why you are doing it. Often the slower worker will see how much more effort his colleague is putting in and will recognize ways to improve his own performance.

If it is the case that an established shelver, who usually gets a satisfactory amount of work done, is beginning to fall short, another type of approach may be called for. A private talk is always a good place to start. You can begin by complimenting her on her consistently good performance and let her know that you are glad to have her as a member of your team. Tell her you have noticed that her work rate has not been as high recently and that you are wondering if there is anything you can do to help. If she tells you she is having a difficulty at home for one reason or another and is feeling really down about it, I suggest that you respond with sympathy and understanding. We all go through periods of personal upheaval from time to time. A person who has been an outstanding worker is likely to be so again once she gets back on an even keel. The fact that you have noticed her distress and are willing to be supportive may help that happen even faster. If your library offers access to any free counseling services, you can remind your employee that this type of help is available to her.

NO LONGER UP TO THE JOB?

Older adults who work as shelvers are generally excellent employees. They have spent years in the workplace and understand what is required of them regarding punctuality, cooperation, and performance. I have had people working for me well into their eighties and would not be surprised to learn that in some libraries, shelvers are still pushing book carts around well past their ninetieth birthday.

However, none of us can last forever. There may come a time when you notice that an employee who has been an active and conscientious worker for several years is slowing down and making mistakes. The last thing you want to do is upset someone by telling him bluntly that it's time to give up his job. It is likely to be a social lifeline for him and quite possibly a reason for getting out of bed in the morning. But if you see evidence of advancing frailty you must act. Begin by letting the person know that he is highly thought of throughout the library. Explain that you and other staff members are concerned about his welfare and ask if there is anything you can do for him.

It is possible that at this stage, your shelver may admit that he feels the job might be getting a little too much for him. He might not have said anything before because he felt you were relying on him. You can assure him that everyone will understand his need to take a well-earned rest. This will then leave the way clear for your senior shelver to resign with dignity. Hold a party, and give him a good send-off.

But what can you do if an employee in these circumstances does not want to admit he is struggling? One response is to move him to tasks that can be done sitting down if the needs of the library are still being met. If this is not an option, you can ask the person to consult with his doctor and bring in some signed proof of his fitness to work. Stress that you are doing this because you are concerned that he might injure himself. Consult your human resources staff and see if there are questions of liability that you can cite as reasons for asking someone to verify his fitness.

Your goal is for the person concerned to have the option of handing in his resignation rather than your requiring him to leave. If he is very reluctant to break off ties to the library, you can always point out that his knowledge of what goes on in the building would make him an ideal volunteer.

WHEN IT GETS PERSONAL

If you ask most supervisors what kind of problems are the most difficult to deal with, I am certain that having to speak to someone about his personal hygiene, or lack of it, would be at the top of everybody's list. You might think that at a time when you can find at least a dozen brands of deodorant in any supermarket or drugstore, you will never come across an instance where it is obvious that someone is not using any. My conversations with other supervisors and my own experience tell a different story. Shelvers do strenuous work and are therefore physically active during their shifts, so sweating while shelving books is not unusual. Moreover, the air often does not seem to circulate as well in areas that are heavily built up with book stacks. So there is a good chance that you will have to speak to a shelver about this at least once in your career. Although not using deodorant is not entirely a matter of discipline, it can disturb the harmony of the working environment in a very direct way, and you cannot allow one person to make everyone else physically uncomfortable.

There is no easy way to tackle this situation, but it is essential to treat the person concerned with as much dignity as possible. Here are some suggestions that may help:

- Talk to him in a private setting. A borrowed office or meeting room would be best.

- Explain that a number of staff members have asked you to mention that they have noticed this person giving off a noticeable odor of sweat. Don't use the word *complaints*, and don't identify these people.

- If you have also noticed the odor, say so.

- If it seems that further explanation is needed, you can point out that it's difficult for people to feel comfortable working alongside someone with a strong body odor and that patrons will be equally put off.

- Ask the person if he thinks he will have any difficulty in eliminating the problem.

It's important to listen with a sympathetic ear during this kind of conversation. Anyone who has this kind of problem brought to his attention is quite likely to get visibly upset. Let him know that you are sorry to have to bring the subject up and don't wish to offend him, but emphasize that you have no choice since it has been mentioned by a number of other staff members. It's possible that someone who has become careless about his personal hygiene is struggling with a severe problem. It's possible he may have been made homeless and be sleeping in a car. If your library has any free counseling services for staff, it may be appropriate to let the person know what is available to help. Or it may just be that the employee has pulled on a used T-shirt a couple of times or is waiting to have his washing machine repaired. Whatever the reason for the difficulty, you still have to make it very plain that you expect him to arrive for all future shifts smelling of nothing stronger than soap.

Before you speak to anyone about this particular problem, I strongly suggest that you make absolutely sure that it has happened more than once. Putting yourself and your employee through this uncomfortable interview because of a single incident will cause unnecessary embarrassment and distress for everyone.

WHAT TO DO ABOUT PARENTS

If you have to speak to one of your teenage shelvers about a disciplinary problem, you cannot always assume that the matter is over and done with just because you have reached agreement with them about what is to happen next. If they go home and mention that you have written them up for a lapse in behavior, you may hear from the parents. It's important to be pleasant and calm if you get a phone call from an irate parent. Listen to everything that the parent wants to say first. In a case like this, it is not unusual to find that a young employee has not given her parents the whole story. Explain that in dealing with their son or daughter, you have followed procedures that apply equally to all library employees and have documentation to back up the action you have taken. Point out that you and their child have already dealt with the matter to your satisfaction and that you are happy to continue working with the teenager. This is usually enough to diffuse the situation.

If you have had no choice but to fire a teenager, the chances of parental feedback are even higher. If a phone call is not enough to satisfy parents' concerns, they may insist on coming in for a face-to-face discussion. At this point you must let your superiors know what is going on and get the human resources department involved. The priority must be to get the matter settled before it can escalate. A meeting of the parents, yourself, and one or more senior staff members should be enough to arrive at a satisfactory resolution.

SOMETIMES YOU HAVE TO FIRE THEM

Taking the final step and dismissing someone is never easy, but if you have given the person every chance to mend his or her ways, you are left with no choice. The rest of your staff will be resentful if appropriate action is not taken against someone who consistently breaches the rules, and rightly so.

Once again, it is vital to follow your library's disciplinary procedure regarding documentation, verbal warnings, and written warnings when you are dealing with any employee who is giving you problems. In this way, you will be able to act immediately when it becomes clear that the only option is dismissal.

Here are some guidelines that I found helpful:

- When you terminate someone's employment, always do it in a private setting, for example, a borrowed office or staff meeting room.
- Have another member of the staff with you, preferably someone from a senior level (in other words, never another page).
- Have all the documentation with you, including dates and times of any incidents, records of meetings, and copies of warning letters.
- State your case clearly and calmly, setting out the events that have led up to this meeting.
- Make it clear that as a result of all that has happened, you cannot continue to employ him.
- If the person is inclined to be argumentative, both you and your supporter can point out that the matter has already been dealt with appropriately on more than one occasion and is no longer open for discussion.
- If the employee is tearful, hand him a tissue and continue with the dismissal process.
- Once any paperwork has been dealt with, escort the person to collect his belongings and then usher him from the building.
- Explain that in the future, he can use all of the library's public facilities but may not enter any staff-only areas.
- Do not allow him to visit his former coworkers on the way out. He has no right to take up your staff's time complaining about his fate.
- Never discuss the specifics of the case with the rest of your staff.

Being on the receiving end of a dismissal is never a pleasant experience, and the employee may become visibly angry or even aggressive during the process. This is why you should never conduct this type of meeting alone. If you have reason to believe that the person being dismissed may become overly agitated, you may want to add an extra safeguard, such as posting a third staff member close by and asking this person to come into the room and ask if all is well if he or she hears shouting. If your library is large enough to employ security personnel, they are ideal for this purpose. The interruption may be enough to calm the situation. Speak to the person as calmly as you can and acknowledge his feelings by saying something like, "I can see that this has upset you." Let him know that you are willing to listen to what he has to say, but make it clear that he cannot continue to shout at you. Ask if he would like to take a few minutes to compose himself. If this does not work, you can try bringing in the most senior staff member available to back you up, at which point the matter will be out of your hands. I hope that you never have to resort to calling police, but if you or other staff members are being threatened, you will have no other choice.

When your other employees see you behaving in a fair, firm, and consistent manner when it comes to discipline, they will understand that you may occasionally have no choice but to show one of their colleagues the door.

It's difficult to regard firing an employee as a positive experience, but neither should you regard it as a personal failure. If you give an employee several chances to change his behavior and he chooses not to, the responsibility is not yours. Sometimes, in spite of all the care you put into your selection process, you will hire someone who turns out to be unsuitable for the job. If you are careful to act only in the best interests of the library and not from any personal motives, then you need not blame yourself when you let someone go.

CHAPTER SIX

PERFORMANCE ASSESSMENT

During my time as a shelving supervisor I was required to prepare a written evaluation of each page's performance six months after hiring. The process had to be repeated at the twelve-month stage and then on every anniversary of the starting date after that. Annual evaluation of staff at all levels is now the norm in most libraries, and so you are likely to face a similar task. The only way to do this well is to have plenty of reliable records you can refer to.

Daily work logs are essential tools for anyone trying to keep track of employees' activities. This is because you need to have a written record of the facts. If you rely only on your memory of events or vague overall impressions of a shelver's work rate, you can quite easily do someone an injustice. Have everyone write a brief account of what they have done at the end of every shift. Ask them to be specific about

- number of carts shelved
- types of materials shelved
- areas shelf-read
- time spent sorting carts for other shelvers, contents checking, or casing materials
- number of times they emptied book drop-off bins
- closing duties (noting the floor or area where these were carried out)
- any problems they have noticed (such as overcrowded areas)

By asking your staff to make honest assessments of the amount of work they are getting done, you also encourage them to ask themselves if they could be doing more.

Read these logs daily (a sample daily log is in the appendix). For convenience, I advise keeping all of them in a centrally placed binder. If you find entries that you think will be especially useful when writing assessments, photocopy them and put them aside in a separate folder that you keep in your desk. For example, if a shelver gets through an outstanding amount of work one day, you can write a note of personal thanks in this person's log.

He will be pleased to have his efforts recognized, and you can keep a copy of that entry to use later in his evaluation. You can also record any favorable remarks that staff from other departments make about any of your employees. If you gather information, favorable or otherwise, in this way throughout the year, you will arrive at the time when you have to fill out the evaluation forms with your work already half done. I also suggest that you let your employees know from the start that you will be using their logs for this purpose and that you want to know about all the good things they are doing. Speak to everyone again shortly before you write assessments and encourage them to give you any further information they think you should have. You can save yourself a lot of work by encouraging them to give you as much direct input as possible.

It is possible, of course, that one or two shelvers may be tempted to give you a slightly inflated account of their achievements, but if you are paying attention to what everyone does daily, not much will get past you. For example, if someone reports that she is shifting the materials in her sections as often as needed, you have only to go and look at the area in question to see if this is true.

You may need to include polite reminders about unfinished tasks in a shelver's log from time to time, but any comments that are more serious in tone need to be delivered face to face and in private. A binder containing everyone's log sheets is much too public for any kind of rebuke. You must deal in a timely manner with legitimate complaints about a shelver's work, but it is better to keep such instances noted in a separate log of your own that remains private.

If you hold meetings of shelvers, and I strongly suggest that you do, keep a record of what is discussed and list the names of those who attend. When assessment time comes around, the page logs, training logs, meeting records, and your own daily notes should give you enough material to make producing evaluations relatively straightforward. Once the evaluations are complete, destroy the old log sheets and any notes you've compiled, or hand them over to human resources to be placed in the shelvers' individual files.

In order to write a performance review, you must have clear ideas about what you expect from the person. When you hire shelvers, you do so because you believe they have abilities and aptitudes that make them well suited to carry out specific tasks. When you come to assess their continued suitability for those tasks, going back to the basic criteria can be helpful:

- Are they punctual?
- Do they consistently turn up for their scheduled shifts?
- Are they always willing to work the hours you require?
- Can they arrange their schedule without needing your intervention?
- Are they cooperative with you and their coworkers?
- Do they tackle jobs without waiting to be asked?

- Can they work without close supervision?
- Do they make an effort to come to page meetings?
- Do they adhere to library policies?
- When appropriate, are they directing members of the public to the members of the library staff who can help them best?
- Are they keeping up with their shelf reading?
- Are their sorting and shelving skills still up to standard?

If you are having doubts about whether one of your shelvers is taking sufficient care about putting materials in the right place, you can ask her to shelve a cart of materials using the training slips. You need to use some tact here. If you don't want to be seen as singling anyone out for this type of retesting, you could ask all employees to do this as a standard part of their assessment. Those who meet your expectations by passing with flying colors will give you yet one more opportunity to write something complimentary about them. And the hope is that those who might have been falling off the standard will be encouraged to start paying more attention to the basics simply because you are giving their skills some scrutiny. Either way, you will have something to discuss during the review.

If you have not prepared evaluations before, I strongly recommend talking to the person you will be submitting them to and asking for some concrete guidelines before you begin. For example, in the spirit of wanting to give your shelvers the recognition they deserve, you may feel inclined to reward the best shelvers with a generous proportion of the highest rates of approval. But it would be disappointing to go ahead and do so, only to find out that the top accolades are meant to be handed out sparingly. Having to then go back over the evaluations and make a large number of changes would be a tremendous waste of your time. Some libraries hold training sessions for staff who have to prepare assessments of other workers, and you should certainly take advantage of those if they are available.

When you are working on the evaluations, be careful not to have the documents lying about in plain sight on your desk. Don't get up and walk away from a computer and leave pages from a review up on the screen either. Shelvers may be only part-time workers, and poorly paid ones at that, but they deserve the same privacy and consideration for their feelings that the rest of the library staff are given when it comes to reviewing their performance. Take the time to go over your individual evaluations with each of your employees in private. If you don't have the luxury of an office, borrow someone else's or use an enclosed meeting room.

If you have not given your staff a chance to look at what you've written about them beforehand, it's a good idea to start the review session by letting them read their individual assessments. Then I recommend that you go over all of the positive and encouraging comments that you have included in the assessment. This should help you both feel more at ease. We all like to be praised, and handing out compliments will make you feel good too.

Once you have gone over all the good points, ask the person you're evaluating if there is anything she would like to talk about. This will give her the chance to start the conversation about any areas where you have suggested that improvements are needed. In my experience, people are often aware of their own shortcomings and may have their own suggestions about how they can improve their performance. If they don't seem to understand why you might be less than satisfied with some aspect of their performance, you need to be explicit. Stick to the facts, and if you have taken frequent notes during the preceding weeks and months, you should have plenty of those. Try to avoid phrases that begin with "you don't" or "you're not." No one is going to react well if you just recite a list of their shortcomings. It's better to use positive statements like, "I know you are willing to do better," or "Can you suggest a way that we can make this work?" At the end of the discussion, you can decide together on what steps your employee is going to take to try and improve her performance. You must also agree on a way of following the matter up and how and when any improvement will be measured.

Any evaluation that you put together should always contain some positive remarks. If you ever find yourself sitting in a room with someone whom you cannot say a good word about, this will say more about you than it will about the person you are reviewing. What it will indicate is that you, as a supervisor, need to start dealing with issues such as discipline and poor performance much sooner.

Today even shelving supervisors are often required to agree on performance goals with employees. This can seem like an unnecessary formality when an individual is working only twelve hours a week, but it must be done. The best way is to keep these goals very simple—for instance:

"Increase the number of page meetings you attend."

"Sign up for two in-house training sessions."

"Review your training log on a regular basis, and shelve a cart of materials from any areas that you have not handled in the past three months."

"Spend thirty minutes a week shelf reading."

In my library, the same assessment form was used throughout the building to measure everyone's performance, including the department heads. But entire sections of it did not seem particularly relevant to the duties that pages and shelvers carried out, and I would have preferred to put my own assessment package together. If you think that the form you are required to use is unsuitable, you could make up one of your own, and see if your library will accept it. (A sample of a shelver performance evaluation document is in the appendix.)

In many libraries, all staff performance assessments are often done at the same time of the year. If you are in charge of a dozen or so employees, having to assess them all at once is nothing short of a nightmare. Talk to your superiors and point out that it will make far more sense for you to review your staff on their start date anniversaries. It's not hard to make a good case for doing this. You are likely to be in charge of more employees than anyone else in the building. Anyone who dreads having to prepare a mere handful of evaluations will surely understand that dealing with a dozen or more at a time is a monumental task, no matter how well prepared you are.

When you have to write a large number of assessments, it can sometimes be difficult to come up with fresh ways of saying things. There are several books that are full of useful phrases for performance evaluations, and you can consult them for help in this area. Here are some titles on the subject that are widely available in public libraries.

> *How to Say It Performance Reviews: Phrases and Strategies for Painless and Productive Performance Reviews*, by Meryl Runion (New York: Prentice Hall Press/Penguin Group, 2006).

> *Perfect Phrases for Performance Reviews: Hundreds of Ready-to-Use Phrases That Describe Your Employees' Performance (from Unacceptable to Outstanding)*, by Douglas Max (New York: McGraw-Hill, 2003).

> *Performance Appraisal Phrase Book: Effective Words, Phrases, and Techniques for Successful Evaluations*, by Cory Sandler (Cincinnati, OH: Adams Media, 2004).

Assessing employee performance is a demanding task for managers at all levels. But you can ease your burden considerably by keeping notes and records on a daily and weekly basis so that when the time comes, you will have plenty of useful and relevant material at your fingertips. As a bonus, a lot of the same information will also come in handy if you are required to write monthly reports (a sample shelving supervisor's monthly report is in the appendix).

CHAPTER SEVEN

WORKING WITH OTHER DEPARTMENTS

To borrow a phrase from Jane Austen, it is a truth universally acknowledged that as soon as you are put in charge of the pages, you will be held directly responsible for the state of every book shelf and, furthermore, a large number of people will feel it is their duty to bring any and all instances of disarray to your immediate attention. You must get used to this and develop constructive ways of responding to what may feel like personal criticism. If someone complains to you about the untidy state of the picture books, for example, you will probably be tempted to lay the blame at the feet of the toddlers who come in and rummage through them daily. A better response might be to arrange to have a shelver go into that area at regular intervals during the day to make running repairs.

If another member of the library staff is frequently giving you criticism about the way your shelvers and pages go about their duties, try not to get defensive. Instead you could thank the person for this concern and ask for a list of any suggestions in writing. However, if you feel that someone is being overly critical for no good reason, take your concerns to your own supervisor. My conversations with other page supervisors over the years have led me to suspect that now and again people complain about shelvers simply because they are an easy target. They are on the lowest rung of the library ladder and can never claim to have finished their work.

If you have just taken over as page supervisor and your predecessor has moved to another job within the library, both of you will have a period of adjustment. She is naturally still going to take an interest in the shelvers she hired, trained, and, until recently, supervised every day. The shelvers too will take a little while to get used to the change. They may even turn to their former supervisor for help or advice if you are not nearby. Time will take care of this dependence, and it is usually not worth getting agitated about, but if a former supervisor is frequently returning to her old haunts and interfering with the way you are trying to run things, you need to act. First, try taking the previous supervisor aside and explaining politely that you understand why she enjoys coming back to visit but that you really need to establish your own authority. You can add that if you find it necessary to seek advice, she is certainly the first person you will turn to. If the situation does not improve after that, you might need to have a word with the person you report to for help.

If the former page supervisor happens to be the person who is now supervising you, persuading her to let go of the reins may be more difficult. You can try waiting a few weeks until her own new duties absorb so much of her time that she is no longer able to take such a close interest in you and your shelvers. If the situation still does not improve, you may have to ask someone at a higher level to intervene.

As the supervisor of shelvers, you will have daily contact with staff in nearly every other department in the library, so it is essential that you and your team are on good terms with all of them. Do as much as you can to ensure that any interaction between one of your shelvers and another staff member is a positive experience:

- Always introduce your new shelvers to as many other library staff as possible, especially those working at reference and inquiry desks.

- When librarians or other staff have to come searching for a book or other item for a patron, make sure your shelvers offer to help them at once, every time.

- Make sure shelvers understand both the scope and the limitations of their duties. For instance, they should not attempt to answer reference questions but should be ready to assist other staff in any way they are asked.

I used to go into the last twenty minutes of adult and youth services department meetings so that any concerns about the pages and their work could be aired in a controlled way. People were more inclined to keep their criticism constructive when speaking in front of a department head and when minutes were being taken. It was not unusual for other members of the same department to disagree with anyone expressing negative views about the shelvers during the meetings, and it was gratifying to have compliments about the pages recorded as well.

I strongly recommend that when you are at these meetings, you ask each department for a list of shelving priorities. If there is a consensus on where the pages should be directing their efforts, this information will help to foster an atmosphere of cooperation.

Be sure to let everyone know when your own page meetings are being held and encourage them to let you know of any concerns that they would like you to mention to your staff. You could also invite heads of other departments, as well as your own supervisor, to drop in from time to time. It will certainly give your shelvers a boost if senior staff members take the time and trouble to tell them in person that their efforts are appreciated. You should also encourage shelvers to speak up and ask questions for themselves during these encounters with management. Someone who does not have to put materials away may not fully realize the frustration and difficulties that can arise if collections are not weeded fast enough and the shelves become too full. Having the chance to voice their concerns in this way will help your staff feel that they are taking part in a useful dialogue. Anything that shows shelvers that they are a vital and appreciated part of the library is worth doing.

Stay as well informed as possible about any changes that other departments are planning to make because they can have a big impact on the way shelvers do their work. Today an increasing number of tasks that used to be done in library technical services departments are being outsourced. New materials often arrive with all the necessary bar codes and labeling and pockets already in place. In order to keep costs down, labels applied outside the library are likely to be standardized. For example, fiction may be identified only by the first eight letters of an author's last name. This is bound to have some impact, as some names will be shortened and will not be as immediately recognizable as when they were spelled in full. You need to know about these changes in advance so you can let your shelvers know what to expect. Maintain close ties with your colleagues in technical services and always express an interest in any plans they have to make changes in packaging or labeling. People who do not have to sort and shelve materials every day are not always aware of the difficulties that can be caused by adding a collection whose identifying marks resemble those of another group of materials too closely. Your goal is to be on such good terms with the people who process new materials that they automatically ask you about changes *before* they get put into effect.

If any major changes are in the offing at your library, such as a change to the floor plans or the adoption of an inventory system such as radio frequency identification, you should let the people doing the planning know that you would like to be involved or at least be kept fully informed. Your reason for wanting to be a part of the process is obvious: it will have a direct impact on you and your staff. Let people know that you want to be well prepared so that you can do your best to ensure that the materials continue to make their way back to the shelves in an efficient and timely manner during and after the changes. Libraries are not static organizations, and it will be much better for you to be seen as willing to take new directions in their stride. If you are seen as cooperative, you stand a much better chance of being consulted in the early stages of any new scheme. You may not agree with everything that is proposed or carried out, but at least you will have set out your thoughts.

When other departments ask to borrow pages for various tasks, do your best to accommodate them. Being cooperative is a required part of everyone's job. In addition, you are more likely to get a sympathetic hearing from your colleagues when you are understaffed and restocking times are creeping up if you have been responsive to their requests in the past.

Another good reason to let your pages get experience in other areas is that these temporary assignments may result in their being offered a job elsewhere in the library. This may not be good news for you in the short term. In the long run, however, it will show that you are capable of selecting and training people who are well worth promoting. It will also encourage other library staff to regard shelvers as potential colleagues and full members of the library family.

CHAPTER EIGHT

LOOKING AFTER THE SUPERVISOR

Many of us find the idea of supervising other people daunting and are not sure if we have the appropriate skills. My advice is to start looking for help as soon as you take on your new responsibilities. (For some people—librarians, for instance—this will not be a promotion but more of an expansion of duties.) The business section of your library is sure to have materials that deal with making the transition to being in charge of other employees. Read them, and draw on the ideas and strategies that seem to fit your situation. I think it is especially important to seek guidance if you are supervising people who were previously your coworkers. It can sometimes be difficult when people who regard themselves as your friends and your equals are slow to adapt to the reality that they are now expected to defer to you during working hours. Companies that specialize in training often hold regional one-day courses on making the transition to being in charge and building up supervisory skills. I attended a couple and found them very useful. Although not everything was relevant to my situation, I was able to bring away half a dozen useful tips and ideas from each session. Increasingly training is available online, and this may be a good alternative if you are not able to take time away from your building.

The most effective thing you can do is to get together with other page supervisors and pick their brains. Shortly after I became a supervisor, a neighboring library sent out invitations to a meeting exclusively for people in charge of pages and shelvers. We were asked to bring any forms, training aids, and assessment tools that we used so that we could pool these resources with the other attendees. In one of the sessions, recruitment and rates of pay were discussed. Supervisors were also invited to speak about any aspects of their jobs they were having difficulties with, so that others could offer possible solutions to their problems. More than forty people attended, and it was an unqualified success. The quarterly meetings rotated around local libraries for a number of years. In 2007 the North Suburban Library System, an organization that offers educational and technical support to the libraries in the northern Chicago suburbs, began working with the area's shelving supervisors to help them set up an online community of practice at the same time they offered the group the NSLS facilities as a central venue. Meetings are now scheduled every three months, a year in advance. If you do not have a supervisors' forum like this in your area, I suggest that you try to start one. There is no substitute for getting together with people who understand the challenges you face and can offer the benefit of their experience. It will do you good to be able to share your problems with a truly sympathetic audience.

If you want to set up a group and hold the first meeting in your own library, you will obviously need to get approval. There are various benefits that you can draw attention to when making your case.

- Your library can be seen as initiating a new area of cooperation with other libraries, which is something your director may like to draw attention to.
- Visiting supervisors will bring ideas from other libraries that may help improve the work flow in yours.
- Your performance as a supervisor will benefit from your exposure to new ideas.

If you are in the suburbs that surround a large city, there will be a number of libraries within easy driving distance, and it will not be hard to set up a session that can be completed in half a day. Friday mornings seem to be a time that most shelving supervisors can manage to get away from their responsibilities. If you go to a supervisor's meeting at another library, be sure to take a tour. If you see anything that could save time and money in your own building, even something that is outside your own area, don't be hesitant about suggesting it to the appropriate person.

If you are in an area where the libraries are distant from one another, a meeting may not be easy to arrange. In this case, an online forum can be useful. Try to determine if there are any regional or state resources that can help you set one up. If you go to conferences for library support staff, you could ask the organizer to set aside a room where shelving supervisors could meet each other and network.

There are never enough hours in the day to sort returned materials and get them back on the shelf. You cannot be everywhere at once, and you must learn to delegate if you are to be effective. Give your pages their own sections to look after, and make them responsible for the shelf reading and general upkeep in those areas.

Some of your pages will know as much about the collections as you do, and possibly even more. It makes a lot of sense to enlist their help with new shelvers once you have overseen the early stages of their training and are satisfied that they have the necessary competence. Shelvers with seniority will appreciate that you value their experience and will be pleased that you are placing your trust in them. If an experienced shelver has not trained anyone before, go to the relevant areas with her beforehand and ask her to show you how she would explain the work to a newcomer. One advantage of having another responsible staff member doing some of the training is that it shows your trainees that paying attention to detail is the usual approach to shelving work, and not just an obsession of yours.

Supervising library pages is often hard work, but it does have rewards (although a large salary may not be one of them). Libraries usually prefer to promote from within, and pages, with their hands-on knowledge of how the library is organized, make excellent candidates for nonprofessional openings in other departments. Pages I hired went on to work in technical services, circulation, and interlibrary loan. Two of them became full-time page supervisors, and one became the personal assistant to the library director. It's always deeply satisfying to see one of the shelvers you hired progress from a part-time job to a full-time career. So is giving a high school student her first job and then watching her develop into a confident and useful employee. Intangible rewards like this are no less important than the money you earn, and learning to appreciate them will enhance your working experience.

Being in charge of others is a challenge, but it's also an opportunity to acquire organizational skills and develop good working relationships throughout your library, and that can benefit you in whatever you decide to do next.

CHAPTER NINE

THE BIG MOVES: YOUR CHANCE TO SHINE

A few years ago when my library was building a large addition, it was necessary to move all of our collections over a period of months, and some of them more than once. The first time that we needed to move all our adult fiction, we hired a firm that specialized in library work. We did not hire them again.

If you know that a similar large-scale expansion or reorganization is going to take place at your library, I urge you to get involved with the planning at an early stage. You and your team of shelvers will be the ones who are most affected if hired movers are brought into the building. I have spoken to several page supervisors who had to spend weeks sorting out the chaos left behind by so-called professionals. It will be far better if you can take an active role in deciding how this work will be done. Not only will the library benefit if the relocation of materials goes smoothly, but you will also have proved that you are capable of undertaking and succeeding at a large-scale project.

WHY IT MAKES SENSE TO DO IT YOURSELF

On the face of it, deciding to move large parts of your collection without the help of professionals sounds foolhardy. After all these people have the equipment and the manpower and have done similar jobs many times before. Why not hire them? Here are several good reasons:

- No one has a greater interest in seeing that the collection ends up in its new home in good order than your own library staff.
- Professional movers do not hire retired librarians to move books. They hire minimum-wage laborers whose grasp of the alphabet or the Dewey system may not be complete.
- Even if they get the books to the right shelf, the smaller details such as correct order and neatness are often overlooked.
- The moving companies usually do not supervise their workers closely enough.

- If books are placed on the wrong shelves or whole sections of books are left out, it's likely that these errors will not be picked up at the time, and the library staff has to sort out the mess.

Another good reason for not hiring outside help is the enormous cost. You are going to be charged at least twelve dollars per hour for each laborer and more for supervisors. It makes little sense to pay to bring in workers who have no knowledge of the materials they are being asked to handle when you have your own experienced shelving staff on site. By using existing library staff and some hired equipment, you can easily cut the cost of a major book moving operation by a third, if not more.

I am going to show you a simple and practical method that will make it possible for you to move large quantities of books and other materials with a minimum of error. It will work equally well if you are moving your collection from place to place on a single site or going from an old building to a new one.

WHERE DO I START?

Before you can begin planning how and where things are going to be moved, you have to know how much material you are dealing with. For the purpose of this exercise, we are going to suppose that you will be moving your existing adult nonfiction collection from its old home to a new area in the recently constructed addition to your library building.

Before we go any further let me make the terms I will be using to describe ranges of bookshelves absolutely clear:

- A *unit* is a vertical arrangement of between three and seven shelves, usually 36 inches wide.
- *Stacks* are rows of units that are attached to each other. They can be single or double sided.

It will not help you to know how many individual books you will be shifting. The only measurement that matters at this stage is the number of shelf inches that the books are currently taking up.

There is no substitute for working your way along each existing stack, measuring the amount of materials on each shelf as you go. If all shelves are completely full, you might be able to get away with just multiplying the number of shelves by their individual length (usually 36 inches), but I do not recommend this. The more time you spend on getting a realistic count of total book inches, the more smoothly moving the collection will go.

It's essential to keep clear and detailed records as you go. You can easily adapt spreadsheet grids to make a plan of each unit and stack. Note the inches of books on each shelf, and make a note of where each section of Dewey numbers begins and ends.

It is also useful to note areas where the shelf heights are different, for example, in places where there are oversize books such as the 700s. Note the total inches for each individual stack, and then add up all the stacks to reach the total number of book inches for the whole adult nonfiction collection.

When you have finished this stage, your thigh muscles will be protesting loudly. (Try lowering yourself slowly from the top shelf to the bottom one a couple of hundred times, and you will know why I mention this.) You might want to split this task with some of your shelvers or other colleagues. It's a good idea to have people work in pairs. One person can measure, while the other notes down the figure for each shelf on a chart. Just be sure everyone realizes how important it is to be accurate. Of course, no matter what you do, your final figure will be off to some degree because patrons will be taking books off the shelves and pages will be putting them back. I will show you how to build in some allowances for this later on.

For this exercise, I am going to assume that the adult nonfiction is currently housed on twenty stacks containing fourteen units of six shelves (forty-two shelves per side, eighty-four shelves per stack). After measuring the amount of materials on each shelf, let's say that you arrive at a figure of 53,760 inches.

WHAT DO I DO WITH THIS RIDICULOUSLY LARGE NUMBER?

Next go to the floor plan of the new building addition or reorganized area and count the number of shelves that will be available to house these materials. Your hope is that it will be a greater number than the shelves they are currently sitting on in the older part of the building. (If it is not, you might want to begin preparing the bonfire for the architect now.)

Let us say that you will have an additional ten book stacks available in the new area. This will give you thirty stacks containing 2,520 shelves. At this stage, you need to remember to factor in any areas where the shelves are spaced more widely to accommodate larger books, in the 700s, for instance. Divide the collection inches total by the number of new shelves available.

$$53,760 \div 2,520 = 21.333 \text{ inches of books per new shelf}$$

To keep things simple, round this figure up to the next inch. This means that you are going to assume that each shelf in the new nonfiction area will carry only 22 inches of books. This will be a nice change from the average of 33 inches that are crammed onto the shelves at the moment.

IS IT REALLY NECESSARY TO TAG THE COLLECTION?

Yes, it is absolutely necessary, for the following reasons:

- Marking the books with prenumbered adhesive tags will ensure that they will arrive on exactly the right shelf in their new home.

- Tagging will give you flexibility in the way that the move can be carried out.
- Tagged sections of books do not have to be moved or reshelved in any particular order. You can have people working at both ends of a collection simultaneously, and in the middle too if you like.

Buy some rolls of colored adhesive tape marked off in numbered sections. (You can obtain them from a company that specializes in moving books.) You will need at least two rolls of each color: one roll to go on the books and the other roll to go on the new shelving. Pick a color (blue, for example), and start at the first book in the 001s. Put the first tag on this book, and then measure the first 22 inches, making sure that you include the first book in this measurement. Put the next tag on the book immediately after the 22nd-inch mark, and continue tagging until you have used up the entire roll. (You will find this job much easier if you wear the roll of numbered tape on a length of cord around your neck.) You can work on your own or in a team of two. When you get to the end of the first roll of tape, switch to a different color. Don't forget to put the matching roll of blue tape in a safe place because it will be essential later.

As you go along, keep a note of the tag numbers that mark the end of each Dewey section—for example:

Dewey 00s	blue tags 0001 to 0023
Dewey 100s	blue tags 0024 to 0075
Dewey 200s	blue tags 0075 to 0156
Dewey 300s	blue tags 0157 to 0301

Note also the changes in tagging tape color:

Dewey 600s	blue tags 0652 to 1000 and yellow tags 0001 to 0043
Dewey 700s	yellow tags 0044 to 0256

You may think that I am going overboard on the detailed note keeping, but you would be wrong. I can guarantee that you will be asked which shelves the 600s will be going to in the new part of the building or where the 900s will start, and if you do as I suggest, you will have all that information at your fingertips. Not only will you astonish your colleagues with your grasp of the situation, but you will boost your own confidence in your ability to get this move done efficiently.

Tagging is one of the most time-consuming aspects of an operation like this, so start as far ahead of your move as is practical. If you have to do it while the library is open, be sure to alert the circulation staff so they can rescue any tags that might be on a book that a patron is checking out.

Once you have finished tagging the collection, you will be able to work out the total number of 22-inch sections of books you have. I can tell you now that it will not equal the number of shelves waiting to receive the books in the new area. There are a couple of reasons for this:

- When you divided the number of shelves into the total inches for the nonfiction collection (2,520 into 53,760), you rounded the resulting figure (from 21.33 inches up to 22) inches make measuring easier.
- During the tagging process, you or the people helping you will have decided that some sets of books should all be on the same shelf, or that there should be a clean break between the end of one set of Dewey numbers and the beginning of the next.
- The 22-inch rule will have been violated slightly several hundred times, and the effects soon add up.

Don't panic! This can be easily fixed.

HOW DO I FIX IT?

If you have ended up with 2,469 tagged sections to go on 2,520 shelves, you have several options. Those 51 "extra" shelves can be used in a number of ways:

- You could choose to have a 6-shelf space between each Dewey number section and use it for display and future expansion purposes. That would take care of 42 shelves.
- With the remaining 11, you could decide to leave the bottom shelves free in those areas of the 600s that deal with medical complaints common in the elderly, and save people from having to bend all the way down for books on arthritis.
- You can adjust your tagging. You could choose to go down to 21 inches from the beginning of the 900s until you have used an additional 51 tags.

I don't recommend the last option. I think it is far better to go into the moving stage with some shelves in hand.

At this point, I recommend that you make plans of all the individual book stacks in the new area so that you can mark exactly where you will be shelving each tagged section of books. If you do this, you will know before you begin moving the collection that it will fit into its new home just as you want it to.

WHAT NEXT?

Circumstances vary from library to library, but at some stage, you may need to take all of the tagged nonfiction books off their original shelving and store them either on or off site. This will be the case if the existing stacks are going to be reused in the new area. There may be a time lapse of several days between the stacks being taken down and reassembled. This is the stage for which you will need to hire a number of large wooden book carts from a moving company. They are sturdily constructed and usually have four shelves per side, each shelf measuring 48 inches. You should check these details with your supplier before working out how many carts you will need.

If you have to store the entire nonfiction collection for a time, then obviously you have to rent enough carts to fit all the books on. You can work out the number you will need by dividing the total book inches (53,760) by the number of inches each cart can hold (8 times 48 equals 384 inches). The answer is 140.

If you do not need to store the books because they are going to be transferred to thirty completely new book stacks, then you will need fewer carts. You can work out how many by calculating how many staff and volunteers you will have available and dividing the number by two. So if you can muster a workforce of one hundred, you will need to hire 50 carts. I recommend that you always have your workforce operating in pairs. The carts are not lightweight, and it also helps to have people keep an eye on each other. Even experienced staff may begin putting books on shelves backward after a while.

If you have to store some of the books but can move the others right away, you need to work out two figures: the number of carts needed to store part of the collection and the number of pairs of people who can be relocating the rest of the books. Depending on the construction and reopening schedule, you can do one of two things. Let's say you need seventy-five carts to store books and twenty-five carts to move the rest. If the new area is ready to receive books and you don't have to dismantle the original stacks right away, you can do your moving first and storage afterward. In this case, hire only seventy-five carts.

The rental for each cart per day will be in the range of eight to ten dollars. You should expect to pay a drop-off fee of at least seventy-five dollars and a similar pickup fee when the company delivers and collects the carts. This payment is often required at the time, by check or in cash, so make the necessary arrangements. Be sure to have as many staff on hand as possible to wheel the carts into the building.

ARE WE READY TO MOVE YET?

Before you begin moving the books to their new location, tag the shelves that are going to house them using the duplicate rolls of colored tape. I can guarantee that at some point while you are tagging, you will accidentally skip a shelf. If you have your detailed plans with you and refer to them frequently, you will very quickly notice any slips you make and be able to put things right. Using the plans also makes it easier to mark the shelves that you have decided to leave empty. When you have finished, each tagged section of books will have a shelf with an identical tag waiting for it.

FIGURE 9.1   *MOVING LABEL SHOWING EXACTLY WHICH BOOKS*
SHOULD BE PLACED ON A SPECIFIC STACK

STACK 1

Dewey No's 001–158.1

Side A   Side B
Blue tags 0001–0039   Blue tags 00040–0081

Shelves with no tags have been left blank on purpose.

It is helpful to put as much information as possible on the ends of the stacks for the benefit of your movers. I recommend numbering the individual stacks and designating the two sides of each stack as A or B. It is also very helpful to put labels on the ends of the stacks that show the tag numbers and tag colors of the books that should be shelved there (see figure 9.1). At no stage of this operation is there such thing as too much information.

AND AWAY YOU GO

Once everything is tagged and labeled, gather your workforce together for a short pep rally. Thank them profusely for agreeing to undertake this monumental task, and then give them a few pointers in the art of moving large quantities of books:

- The books must go from an old shelf to a moving cart and then from a moving cart to a new shelf without ever deviating from their correct order. It is all too easy for handfuls of books to get out of sequence when they are being taken from a shelf by one person and then passed over to someone else to be loaded on the cart. Give a short demonstration to get your point across.

- Only complete tagged sections are placed on the carts. It will do no good at all to cram the first half of a section into the last space on a cart and put the rest of it on a different one. Without the tag, the books will not be easily to identify and could get lost. The aim of the exercise is to get the tagged books to their correct new home. Leaving a few gaps on the moving carts does not matter at all.

- Fully explain the labels on the ends of the stacks. Let your helpers know that you have plans of all the stacks on paper and can easily confirm where every tagged section of books belongs. Encourage them to ask you if they have even the slightest doubt about where they are going to put things. Remember, you have all the answers!

There are also things for you to pay attention to in this massive undertaking:

- If you are using both library personnel and volunteers, it is essential that you pair a staff member with a volunteer.
- Any staff member who is paired with a volunteer must have a solid grasp of the basic points of shelving.
- Board members or pairs of volunteers should not work together because they do not have a working knowledge of your library's collections and are likely to make mistakes. Since one of the main aims of this exercise is to keep errors to a minimum, you need to be insistent on this point.
- Children of board members or staff should not be entrusted with any shelving, even if their parents think it will be a good idea if they help.
- It is also a good idea to have at least one other person in your building who has as complete a grasp of the whole operation as you do. That way, if you are sick on the day of the move, it won't all come to a grinding halt.

Once you have explained how the system works, people start moving books to several areas of the new shelving at the same time. This will be easier than having everyone try to maneuver carts into the same few aisles at once. If you have done your homework, the move should go quite smoothly. As soon as you have one or two stacks filled, you can send a team to double-check that the tags on the books and the shelves match.

HOW DO I PERSUADE MY COLLEAGUES THAT THIS IS A GOOD IDEA?

You can make huge savings by using library staff and hired carts, and this is always going to be a powerful argument. You can also stress that hardly any remedial work will be needed once the books are in their new home. Everyone has heard unsettling stories about library personnel having to spend hours sorting out the shambles left behind after professional movers have been let loose on a collection.

Working together on a project like this can be a pleasurable experience. If you are moving a large part of your collection, you will probably be closed to the public for a time and will have a chance to build up a different kind of working atmosphere. Everyone from the director down can wear their jeans and roll up their sleeves! Make sure that lunches are catered in for everybody. You will be saving thousands of dollars, so don't begrudge a few hundred to keep the workers happy and energetic. Those who cannot push a book cart can form the catering team. It is also a good idea to have a team at the front door to greet and mollify those patrons who won't have read the notices and flyers about the closure.

SOME QUESTIONS YOU MIGHT HAVE

Can I move more than one collection at a time safely?

> You certainly can. When our library was closed to rearrange itself within a newly enlarged building, we moved every collection we owned using the measure and tag method.

What if I have to use the same color tape on different types of books?

> This shouldn't be a problem. Just make sure they are hard to confuse. For instance, if you used green tape on such diverse collections as adult mysteries, youth nonfiction, and Russian language books, there would be almost no chance of accidental mingling.

What if I have to start tagging the new shelves out of sequence and I need the highest numbers on my duplicate roll of tagging tape first?

> I had to do this more than once myself. You will need to store the low-numbered tags on some old laminated posters or similar material. I found that the tags would safely stick and restick at least three times.

Is all this planning and paperwork really necessary?

> Yes. If you are going to ask a sizeable workforce to move large quantities of materials from one place to another and have it all end up in the right place, you need to know exactly what you are doing. More important, you need to be able give people exact instructions and have them feel confident that you are totally in control.

If you are tempted to plan a move of your own and are in need of additional encouragement, feel free to e-mail me at ptunstall@itpld.lib.il.us.

FORMS AND TOOLS

Selected appendix forms can be found on the book's website at www.ala.org/editions/extras/tunstall10108.

VACANT POSITION SIGN

Signs like this one often bring in applicants. Put them in as many locations in the library as possible, including the areas next to the juvenile materials.

BOOKTOWN PUBLIC LIBRARY

VACANT POSITION

LIBRARY PAGE/SHELVER

This is a part-time position

12 hours per week

Main duties are sorting and shelving library materials

Evenings and weekend hours only

Starting pay is $7.75 per hour

Pick up an application form at the circulation desk

or at any reference desk

ADDITIONAL INTERVIEW QUESTIONS

Interview questions can be found on page 6. Here are some more that you may like to use:

Have you worked with the public before?

Do you like working with the public?

Have you worked in a library before?

What level of pay are you expecting?

Have you worked around children?

What experience do you have with computers?

What do you like to read?

Are you prepared to be flexible about which days of the week you could work?

Shelvers can expect to be very busy for their entire shift each time they come in. How do you feel about that?

When you are handling library materials, you have to pay attention to detail all the time. Do you think you will be able to do this?

Why do you think you would like this job?

ALTERNATIVE SHELVING QUIZ

Here is another applicants' quiz.

SHELVING QUIZ

Please read the instructions for each section carefully before answering.

Dewey Numbers

Put the numbers in the sections below in ascending order. Use the numbers 1–10 to show the sequence.

SECTION 1		SECTION 2		SECTION 3	
005	___	347.7364	___	641.5459	___
081	___	347.5052	___	641.302	___
914	___	347.7304	___	649.29	___
568	___	347.3744	___	641.5384	___
614	___	347.252	___	641.5830	___
505	___	347.373	___	649.302	___
212	___	347.5025	___	641.573	___
658	___	347.7344	___	641.562	___
811	___	347.7544	___	641.592	___
641	___	347.7342	___	641.5471	___

Alphabetical Order

Put the names and titles in the following sections in alphabetical order. Use the numbers 1 to 10 to show the sequence.

SECTION 1	SECTION 2	SECTION 3 (TITLES)
___ Steel, Danielle	___ Marshall, John	___ *Gone with the Wind*
___ Parker, Robert B.	___ McCormick, Joseph	___ *Catch-22*
___ Brown, Sandra	___ Marshall, Keith	___ *East of Eden*
___ Kellerman, Faye	___ MacDonald, Roy	___ *The Lord of the Rings*
___ Picoult, Jodi	___ Marshall, George	___ *Catcher in the Rye*
___ Gregory, Phillipa	___ Marshall, Andrew	___ *The Thorn Birds*
___ Patterson, James	___ MacGregor, Hamish	___ *The Far Country*
___ Koontz, Dean	___ McConnell, Sean	___ *To Be the Best*
___ Gabaldon, Diana	___ Marshall, Charles	___ *David Copperfield*
___ Cornwell, Patricia	___ McCormack, Francis	___ *Advise and Consent*

SAMPLE LETTER: THANKS BUT NO THANKS

Send this to anyone you would *never* employ.

Booktown Public Library
123 Chapter Lane
Booktown IL 45678

Freddie Knott-Hired
111 Shady Lane
Booktown IL 56789

November 5, 20XX

Dear Freddie,

Thank you for submitting an application for the shelving position and for taking the time to come in for an interview.

Unfortunately, I am not able to offer you employment. This decision was made after a thorough review of all the candidates.

I appreciate the interest you have shown in the library and would like to take this opportunity to wish you every success in the future.

Sincerely,

Paige Carter
Shelving Supervisor

SAMPLE LETTER: NO THANKS THIS TIME

Use this if you have many good candidates and have to turn someone down whom you *would* employ at another time.

Booktown Public Library
123 Chapter Lane
Booktown IL 45678

Sarah Wright-Stuff
222 Pleasant Place
Booktown IL 56789

November 5, 20XX

Dear Sarah,

Thank you for submitting an application for the shelving position and for taking the time to come in for an interview.

The standard of applicants was high, and it has not been easy to make a final decision. Unfortunately, I am not able to offer you employment at this time, but your application will be kept on file for one year.

I appreciate the interest you have shown in the library and would like to wish you every success in the future.

Sincerely,

Paige Carter
Shelving Supervisor

APPOINTMENT LETTER

Booktown Public Library
123 Chapter Lane
Booktown IL 45678

Scott Shelver
101 Suburbia Lane
Booktown IL 56789

November 5, 20XX

Dear Scott,

Congratulations on your appointment to the library staff.

As we have agreed, your starting date will be November 15, 20XX. Please report
to me at the circulation desk at 5:00 p.m. on that day for orientation and a
general introduction to the library staff. Your job title will be Library Page 1, with
a beginning pay rate of $_____ per hour. You will work an average of 12 hours per
week, with your schedule to be agreed on in advance.

At the time of your orientation, you will be asked to complete federal and state tax
withholding forms and the Employee Eligibility form. You will also be given a copy of
your job description. Please read it carefully. I will review your specific duties with
you at that time. You will be asked to sign the job description once we have reviewed
it together.

I would like to take this opportunity to welcome you to the library staff. We are
all looking forward to working with you and to helping you become a part of our
community service team.

Sincerely,

Paige Carter
Shelving Supervisor

TRAINING SLIP

I recommend the use of training slips when new shelvers are tackling their first few carts. The slips should be brightly colored and have your library name and logo on them so that there is less chance of their being thrown away.

> **Booktown Public Library**
> **123 Chapter Lane**
> **Booktown IL 45678**
>
> **TRAINING SLIP**
>
> **Shelver in training.**
>
> **This book can be checked out.**
>
> **Circulation staff: Please return this slip**
> **to the shelving supervisor.**
>
> **Booktown Library**
> **Read for your Life!**

PAGE JOB DESCRIPTION

These are some general features that can be included on a shelver's job description.

Booktown Public Library Job Description

Position: Page 1

Hours per week: 12

Supervisors: Shelving Supervisor, Senior Pages

General Description

Sorting and shelving library materials and performing other tasks as assigned. The duties for this position include, but are not limited to, the following:

- sorting and shelving all library materials
- emptying book drops
- contents checking returned AV items
- shelf reading
- shifting collections as necessary
- closing and cleanup procedures
- attending meetings
- participating in training sessions
- assisting patrons within agreed limits

Skills Required

- must be able to file library materials alphabetically and numerically
- must have the physical ability to push and pull loaded book carts
- must be able to bend, stretch, and kneel
- must be able to climb on, and balance on, a kick stool
- must be able to communicate verbally and in writing with other library staff and with the public
- must have the ability to follow verbal and written instructions
- must be able to work without direct supervision

Other Requirements

- must be available to work evenings and weekends as required
- must be willing to work with others and be cooperative with all library staff
- must be willing to carry out additional duties not already listed above

DAILY PAGE WORK ASSIGNMENTS

Date:

PAGE	SHELVE	CONTENTS CHECK	BINS	FIRST FLOOR CLOSING	SECOND FLOOR CLOSING
DAYTIME					
EVENING/WEEKEND					

Notes for today: Don't forget to finish up your shelf reading for the week!
It's payroll on Monday! Please fill out your time sheets.

DAILY LOG

Name: _____

Date: _____

Sections shelved: _____

Number of carts shelved: _____

Shelf reading (section and time spent): _____

Contents checking (show time spent): _____

Bins emptied: _____

Closing/cleanup: _____

Other: _____

Questions?

_____

_____

_____

Supervisor's comments

_____

_____

_____

SHELVING SUPERVISOR'S MONTHLY REPORT
NOVEMBER 20XX

STAFF

Two new shelvers were hired this month.

Joe Stackwalker started work on November 6 and will work mainly evening and weekend shifts. His primary sections will be adult fiction and computer books.

Marge Booker began work on November 20 as a daytime shelver. Her main focus will be AV materials.

Mark Record, senior shelver, left the department on November 13 to begin a new job in Technical Services.

Shirley Reliable was promoted to senior shelver and will take responsibility for the adult nonfiction 300s and 600s.

COLLECTIONS

Materials for the following special collections were pulled and displayed.

Thanksgiving (youth)

Holiday cooking (adult)

Ongoing special youth collections included Explorers, Native Americans, and Autumn and Apples

SHELF READING

Sections completed this month:

001 through 158.3

333 through 354.5

512 through 560

613 through 615

Adult Fiction J through L

Large-Type Fiction A through M

Youth Fiction P through R

Picture Books S through U

Meetings

Pages meetings were held on November 21 at noon and at 6:30 p.m.

I went to the Page Supervisor's quarterly meeting at Wordsville Library on November 16.

Agendas for both the above meetings are attached.

I also attended the Adult and Youth Services monthly meetings.

Paige Carter
December 1, 20XX

CONDUCT AGREEMENT

Supervisor name: _____

Employee name: _____

Date: _____

Behavior causing concern: _____

Action employee will take: _____

How improvement will be monitored: _____

Date of next meeting: _____

Outcome: _____

Further action (if required): _____

SHELVER PERFORMANCE EVALUATION

BOOKTOWN PUBLIC LIBRARY

Name: _____

Job Title: _____

Start Date: _____

Evaluation Period: _____

Key: 5 = Excellent; 4 = Very Good; 3 = Satisfactory; 2 = Must Improve; 1= Unacceptable

Works all scheduled shifts and arrives on time.

Rating: (circle one)   5   4   3   2   1

Comments:

Work is accurate and thorough on a consistent basis.

Rating: 5   4   3   2   1

Comments:

Assigned tasks are carried out in the allotted time.

Rating: 5   4   3   2   1

Comments:

Organizes tasks well and makes good use of time at work in general.

Rating: 5   4   3   2   1

Comments:

Works well without direct supervision.

Rating: 5   4   3   2   1

Comments:

Accepts change in procedures and assigned tasks.

Rating: 5   4   3   2   1

Comments:

Cooperates with other staff members and deals effectively with the public.

Rating: 5   4   3   2   1

Comments:

Communicates well with supervisor, in writing and verbally.

Rating: 5   4   3   2   1

Comments:

Employees

Please sign below to indicate that you have reviewed and discussed your performance evaluation with your supervisor. Signing this document does *not* indicate that you agree with the comments made about you.

Employee Comments (this section is optional)

Employee Signature: _____

Date: _____

Supervisor Signature: _____

Date: _____

Department Head Signature: _____

Date: _____

PAGE/SHELVER MANUAL

BOOKTOWN PUBLIC LIBRARY

**Everything you wanted to know about being a shelver
but were afraid to ask.**

Welcome to Booktown Public Library. We are pleased to have you join our staff. Your responsibility is to see that all library materials are in their proper place so that other staff and members of the public will be able to find them easily.

Everyone has "new job jitters." It is perfectly normal at the beginning to doubt that you will fit in, or like the job, or be able to perform well. Things will be confusing at first, as there is a lot to learn, but you will be given training for all the tasks that you are expected to carry out. Please feel free to ask questions any time that you do not completely understand what you have been asked to do.

Please take your copy of this manual home and read through it. If you need to refer to the manual while you are at work, a reference copy can always be found on the shelving supervisor's desk.

SCHEDULE

Your hours will be scheduled one month at a time. *Daytime pages* will have their hours assigned to them by the supervisor. They will normally be weekday hours, but you may be asked to cover an evening or weekend closing if the need arises. *Weekend and evening pages* will schedule themselves according to seniority. Below are a few guidelines concerning scheduling:

- You are expected to work an average of 23 hours per pay period.
- No session should be shorter than 2 hours.
- There should be at least four pages working every shift.
- All evening and weekend pages are expected to work one Friday, one Saturday, and one Sunday per month (unless you have a specific arrangement with the page supervisor).
- You cannot work more than two Sundays per month.
- No more than two Saturdays are to be worked in one month.
- The maximum gap allowed between sessions is four days, but this is not recommended. Aim for a balanced schedule.
- If for some reason you cannot work a scheduled session, you are expected to try to trade sessions with another page. You must inform the supervisor of such trades.

SALARY

You are paid by the hour with biweekly pay periods. Record your hours on both the individual and master time sheets at the *end* of each working day. Time must be recorded in increments of not less than 15 minutes. At the end of each pay period, completed individual time sheets must be submitted to your supervisor. Payments will appear in your bank account every other Thursday.

CONDUCT

1. Please arrive on time. Call if you are ill or know you are going to be late. The supervisor's direct line number is 555-1234. If you are calling when the library is open, you can use the regular phone number, which is 555-6789. *Unexcused absences are grounds for dismissal.*

2. The library has dress guidelines that all employees are expected to follow. Remember that you are working in view of the public. Cut-off pants, tube or halter tops, miniskirts, and sports outfits are not to be worn. Revealing or grubby clothing in general is not appropriate, nor are T-shirts with offensive or suggestive logos. Shorts are not allowed. If your clothing does not meet with approval, you will be sent home on your own time to change. For safety reasons, pages are not permitted to wear open-toed sandals.

3. Refer all patrons to appropriate library staff members when you are asked anything other than directions to an area.

4. Be courteous, pleasant, and businesslike at all times.

5. Unnecessary conversation with other staff members delays work, may disturb patrons, and provokes criticism of the library. It should be avoided.

6. Both visits and phone calls from friends are strongly discouraged. The staff lounge telephone may be used for important outgoing personal calls during your break.

7. Personal music players and cell phones are not to be used while you are working.

8. When your supervisor is absent, directions and instructions from senior staff members are to be followed. If there is any confusion or contradiction, consult your supervisor as soon as possible.

9. Instructions from adult members of other departments concerning matters related to those departments are to be followed.

10. Pages do not give instructions to anybody else. This includes other pages.

LIBRARY PRIVILEGES

As a member of the library staff, you are entitled to certain privileges:

1. *Breaks.* You may take a fifteen-minute break when you work four hours or more at a time. Let your supervisor or another senior staff member know when you leave and when you return. All food and drink *must* be consumed in the staff lounge.

2. *Meals.* When you work more than five consecutive hours, you must take at least a half-hour meal break on your own time. Bring your own food. Only the food put out on the tables in the staff lounge is community property.

3. *Staff Lounge.* You may use the staff lounge for breaks and meals. Please remember to clean up after yourself.

4. *Borrowing Privileges.* All books or materials you wish to take out of the building must be checked out. Fines are not charged for overdue materials, but loan periods should be observed. You are responsible for the replacement of damaged or lost materials.

5. *Photocopy Machines.* Free use of the photocopier machines for personal use should be kept to a minimum.

VACATIONS

You will not receive a paid vacation, but time off can be arranged with your supervisor. Requests for time off should be made as far in advance as possible.

REVIEWS

Your first review will take place after you have worked six months. After that, reviews will be done close to your employment anniversary date.

GENERAL GUIDELINES FOR SHELVING BOOKS

You have two main duties as a shelver in the library: keeping all materials generally in order and making sure every book is in the right place. Before you are let loose among the book stacks, you will undergo a period of training with your supervisor. When you have shown that you have a good understanding of what is required, you will be expected to work with a minimum of supervision. If you are unsure about where an item should be shelved, ask for help. If you are ever unsure about anything, ask to have it explained again. Keep asking until you are sure you understand. There is no place for guesswork when you are shelving library materials! You will need to keep the following guidelines in mind:

1. Books are fascinating. While shelving, you will come across the hundreds that are new to you, and the temptation to read or scan them will be strong. Resist the temptation! Reading on the job cannot be permitted; it would slow the rate at which the books are returned to the shelves. You may set aside anything that you want to check out to read on your own time, but you *must* check it out on the same day. Stray books found stashed around the library will be returned to the shelves.

2. Shelve accurately. There is only one correct place for each item. Accuracy is more important then speed, which you will come with experience. When you begin shelving, take a look along the shelf where you are about to place a book. Make sure you are not misplacing the book by putting it next to another misplaced book. Reshelve any books that you find are out of place.

3. Straighten as you shelve. Your supervisor should be able to tell where you have been working because the area will look neater than it did before you started. Push books forward neatly on the shelves. Push bookends into

place to hold all the books on a shelf upright. Pick up and shelve books that have been left on the floor. Patrons often leave piles of books at the ends of shelves, and it is your job to put them away.

4. Do not overcrowd the shelves. Keep books evenly arranged on the shelves. If you find yourself having to cram or wrestle books into place, then you will need to shift books from an overfilled shelf to one where there is some space (either above or below). Sometimes this will mean extensive shifting to get the room you need. *It must be done!*

5. Identical books should always be shelved next to each other. If you ever find identical books with different call numbers, bring them to the attention of your supervisor or the librarian at the reference desk. This may be a cataloging error and will need to be corrected.

6. Do not attempt to shelve materials that are badly torn (inside and outside), have loose spines (i.e., inside detaching from cover), are missing spine labels, have unreadable spine labels, or are generally in poor condition. Notify your supervisor of any such materials or leave a signed and dated note on her desk that explains the problem. If you find any books that have been vandalized, check to see if the damage has already been noted on the pocket inside the front cover. If it has not, again notify your supervisor.

7. Never sort more books than you can shelve. If for any reason you are unable to finish shelving a cart of books, return the books to the sorting shelves.

8. Always park your cart at the end of a stack so that it takes up as little aisle space as possible.

9. The following items must never be shelved:

     materials from other libraries

     materials labeled "outreach" or "bookmobile"

     materials with an orange interlibrary loan sticker

   If you come across any of these materials, bring them to your supervisor's attention.

10. Youth Service books and materials are never to be shelved on the second floor. If you find any of them on the second floor, take them to a circulation clerk when you finish what you are doing. The circulation clerk can then make sure that the material was properly checked in.

Fiction

1. All fiction books are arranged alphabetically according to the author's last name.

2. Books by authors having the same last name are arranged alphabetically by the author's last and then first name. For example:

     Collins, Jackie comes before Collins, Joan

3. All abbreviations, whether in the author's name or book title, must be treated as though they were spelled out in full. For example:

     St. John would come before Salinger

     Mr. Rogers would come before Morris

     Dr. Dolittle would come before *Doctor on Call*

4. Books by the same author are shelved alphabetically by the first significant word in the title. This means you ignore the "A," "An," or "The" *only* if it is the first word in a title. The following are in the correct order:

Author	Title
Jones, B.	*Equal Measures*
Jones, B.	*An Extreme Remedy*
Jones, B.	*The Long Road*
Jones, B.	*Sudden Death*
Jones, B.	*An Untimely End*

Fiction Rules Specific to Youth Service Materials

1. Fiction books are labeled with a "J" and the first three letters of the author's last name. For example, a fiction book by R. L. Stine would be labeled "J/STI."
2. Young Adult Fiction books are labeled like fiction books with the addition of the letters "YA" and a blue dot on the spine just above the label.
3. Picture Books, Easy Readers, Youth Paperbacks, and YA Paperbacks are shelved alphabetically by the author's last name.

Fiction Rules Specific to Adult Materials

1. All fiction is shelved by author and then by title within the various categories. These include: Fiction, Mysteries, Science Fiction, Short Stories, Westerns, Large Print, and Foreign Language.
2. In general, Adult Paperbacks are shelved in their own separate area according to genre (Romance, Mystery, General Fiction) and are marked with genre stickers and large red spine labels with the first letter of the author's last name. Some "trade" paperbacks *do* belong on the shelves with the hardback books, and the labeling indicates this.

Nonfiction

Each subject classification in the Dewey system is represented by a unique number. As the classification grows more specific, digits are added to the original three-digit number in the form of decimals. This is referred to as the *call number*. Generally the more digits there are after the decimal point, the more specific the subject is. Nonfiction books are shelved according to their numerical value. Following is a list of guidelines to use when shelving books:

1. Nonfiction books are arranged according to their Dewey number, proceeding from left to right from top shelf to bottom shelf in order of *increasing* numerical value. For example: Books having the numbers 629.13, 629.013, 629.031, 629, and 629.132 are arranged as follows: 629, 629.013, 629.031, 629.13, and 629.132.
2. Books having the same number are arranged alphabetically within the number according to the author's last name. For example:

J/570   CAR(Carlson)

J/570   CAR(Carrick)

J/570   CAR(Carter)

J/570   CRA(Crane)

J/570   CRA(Crawford)

3. Books having the same number and the same author are shelved alphabetically by the title.

4. Although biographies are considered nonfiction material, they are *not* shelved numerically. They are arranged alphabetically by the name typed on the spine label. If there is more than one biography about the same person, they are arranged alphabetically by author.

5. All *reference* books are nonfiction and never leave the library. They should be replaced on their shelves in the reference section as soon as possible.

Nonfiction Rules Specific to Youth Service Materials

1. General Nonfiction books are labeled with a "J" before the call number.

2. Biographies are labeled with "J/B/Name."

3. Reference books are labeled "J/R" before the call number.

Nonfiction Rules Specific to Adult Materials

1. In the largest reference section, the materials have yellow and red "Reference" labels. In other sections (Business Reference or Consumer Affairs tables) they have a variety of labels and/or large dot stickers. They are all shelved numerically in their various areas.

2. Reference books with large red dots belong behind the Adult Services reference desk and should always be returned there.

Special Collections: Youth Services

Nonfiction. Nonfiction books are labeled with a "J," the call number, and the first three letters of the author's last name. For example, a book by Tony Phillips, with the call number 796.6483, would be labeled "J/796.6483/PHI."

Reference Books. Reference books can be recognized by a "J/R/" followed by the call number and letters. They also have a yellow reference sticker just above the label. Reference books should be reshelved immediately.

Biographies. Biographies are labeled with a "J/B/" and the name of the person the biography or autobiography is about, not necessarily the author. For example, a book about Sojourner Truth would be labeled "J/B/TRUTH."

Picture Book Paperbacks. Picture book paperbacks have a green label with a star on them. They are not shelved in any particular order.

Cardboard Books. Cardboard books have a star on the spine. They are not shelved in any particular order.

Foreign Language. Foreign language books are labeled in the same way as their English counterparts, with the addition of the name of the language and a blue foreign language sticker. Foreign language books are sorted alphabetically by language group. Each group is then organized in a progression of picture books, easy readers, fiction, nonfiction, young adult fiction, and nonfiction. Use the same shelving methods as you would with English materials.

Parent-Teacher. Parent-Teacher books are labeled like nonfiction books with the addition of the letters PT and a yellow dot.

New Books. New books are those that are less than four months old and they belong on the "New Books" display shelves. Colored tape on the spine indicates which month they began circulating.

Youth Service Magazines and Comics. Both magazines and comics should have an orange dot indicating they belong in Youth Services. Check magazines and comics for condition. If these materials are damaged or older than six months (magazines), bring them to your supervisor's attention. Comics are not shelved in any particular order but do need to be kept neat.

Special Collections: Adult Services

New Books. New fiction and nonfiction books that are less than four months old are shelved in a separate area. New nonfiction books are marked with a fourteen-day sticker. All new books have colored tape on the spine indicating when they were first put in the collection. After six months, they are taken off the "new book" shelves and added to the general collection. You are asked to check the dates in these books when you handle them and place them on a designated cart for processing. The required dates and corresponding tape color will be posted.

Newspapers and Circulating Magazines. Back numbers of magazines and newspapers require daily shelving. Use of these materials is heavy on weekends, so they require extra attention on Monday mornings. Usually this area is assigned to a shelver as an area of primary responsibility. If that person is not in, anyone who has time should check to see if there are any magazines waiting to be shelved.

Newspapers are shelved in date order, and the shelves they belong on are clearly marked. Please fold all papers neatly, and always check that you are returning them to a section that is in correct date order. Any papers in need of repair should be placed on the supervisor's desk with a signed and dated note. Do not reshelve damaged materials.

Magazines are shelved alphabetically by title. They are heavily browsed, and patrons are often not careful about where they put materials back, so check each section carefully as you are putting them away. Magazines should be shelf-read at the same intervals as other materials.

Audiovisual Collections

Movies: DVD and Blu-ray. Movies are split into various genres and marked with colored dots accordingly. These are all labeled with a letter of the alphabet, which is the first letter of the first word of the title. They are shelved within their letter groups but do *not* have to be further organized within those groups.

Movies: Foreign with English Subtitle. These are shelved in a separate section. Language groups are arranged alphabetically. Within each language, the movies are grouped alphabetically by title.

Movies: Foreign Language Collections. These movies do not have English subtitles and are shelved upstairs with the foreign language collections. The label indicates which language the movie is in.

TV Series: DVD. These are organized by title alphabetically. They do *not* have to be further organized by series or volume number.

Kids' DVDs. These are shelved by alphabet letter groups and do *not* have to be put in any further order.

CD-ROM Kits. These are all hung in green bags and are organized by Dewey number. The label side of the bag should hang to the right.

CDs. These are separated into different types of music. Within these groups they are organized alphabetically according to their labels. All the information required to shelve these items can be found on the label.

Audiobooks: Youth. Books on tape and CD and digital books should be shelved with their printed counterparts. Their labels indicate which section they belong to.

Audiobooks: Adult. Books on tape or CD and digital books are in separate collections. They are labeled as if they were books and shelved in their various genre groups accordingly.

SHELF READING PROCEDURE

It's the goal of the library (and the shelving staff in particular) to have every item in its correct place. Accurate shelving is key, and so is regular shelf reading.

- You will be asked to complete at least 30 minutes of shelf reading in your regularly assigned sections each week.
- Pull the first book forward to the front edge of the shelf.
- Scan the label to ensure the book is in the correct place.
- Double-check the first and last books on each shelf to make sure the sequence continues correctly.
- Reshelve any out-of-place items.
- Shelf-read AV collections with the same care as you do books.
- Pull any items that are damaged or need new labels, and put them on the shelving supervisor's desk.
- Record the author/title or the call number of the last item you check in the shelf reading log each time.

CLEANUP PROCEDURES

Finish shelving your materials, and return carts to Circulation approximately 30 minutes before the library closes. Then go to your assigned floor to start cleanup. Begin earlier if the department needs it! Start with one corner of the room, and work your way around the entire room.

Up-to-date lists of the closing procedures can be found on the shelvers' notice board and are also kept at the reference desks on each floor.

Contents Checking

1. DVDs. Check that titles and call numbers match on the case and discs.
2. CDs. Check and match call numbers on case and disc (and on booklet if there is one). If it is a boxed set, make sure that all the discs have been returned. Check the playing surface of CD for signs of defacement or damage.
3. Audiobooks. Check that call numbers match on cassettes or CDs and cases. Check that the correct number of cassettes or CDs has been returned. Check each tape/CD for damage.
4. AV kits/CD-ROM kits. Check that the contents of the bag match the items listed on the label.
5. Magazines. Check these for damage and put them on the supervisor's desk if they need repair.

PLEASE NOTE: If any of the above items are returned as damaged or with items missing, they must not be placed on a cart to be checked in. They must end up on the "New Snag" shelf accompanied by a "Snag Tag." This tag must show your initials, the call number of the item, and a brief explanation of the problem.

EMPTYING OUTSIDE BOOK DROP

-   Retrieve both the key and the empty book bin. Make sure the tag on the book bin reads "Outside Book Drop."
-   Open the lock, and pull out the full book bin.
-   Slide the empty book bin into place, making sure the *handle is facing you.*
-   Close and lock the book drop.
-   *Never sit on the book bin*, as this can cause damage.
-   When you enter the library, replace the keys immediately.
-   The book bin can then be emptied on to the check cart in the usual manner.
-   Make sure the "Outside Book Drop" tag gets moved to the sorting cart's pocket.
-   Return the empty book bin. The designated times for emptying the bin are on the notice board. Please initial the list each time you complete the task.

INDEX

You may also be interested in

Writing and Publishing: If you are interested in writing or reviewing for the library community or publishing a book, or if you need to write and publish for tenure, then *Writing and Publishing* is for you.

Public Libraries Going Green: This is the first book to focus strictly on the library's role in going green, helping you with collection development, disposal, and recycling issues; green equipment, technology, and facilities; programming ideas; ways to get the community involved in the process; and more.

Coaching in the Library, Second Edition: Experienced librarian and coach Ruth Metz outlines a focused and results-oriented plan for achieving the best results from staff members through a coaching style of management.

Fundamentals of Library Supervision, Second Edition: Two experienced library managers explain how to create a productive workplace as they weave expert advice and commentary into an easy-to-use resource. This revised edition focuses on day-to-day, real-world practices.